Digital Branding & Social Media Marketing for Farmers Market Businesses:

Grow Your Audience, Build Your Brand, and Make Social Media Work For You

William (Bill) Davenport

DEDICATION

To my wife Barbara. Without your love and support, allowing me to chase
my passion of connecting farms, artisans, and producers with our local
community, none of this would be possible. You are my rock and the calming
voice in this crazy thing called life. I am forever thankful to you.

To my kids: Alexis, Brianna, Dani May, Reagan Grace, and Saylor Louise, it's
because of you that I am passionate about connecting local communities to
local farmers, growers, producers, and makers. There is magic in our
communities, that I hope strengthens and grows, so that this connection isn't
lost as you grow older, so that you can experience it and help nurture it. I am
forever thankful for you.

Table of Contents

ACKNOWLEDGMENTS

This book wouldn't have happened without many people encouraging me along the way! My Wife, My Momma, fellow Navy Chief Alicia, and friend Burnie have been instrumental in keeping me going with my farmers market endeavours, including this book.

A huge THANK YOU to all the amazing vendors that come out to the markets and share the good and the bad about their market day with me. You truly inspire me to find ways to make us all successful. There are many, MANY more people who have touched me, inspired me, and encouraged me, too many to name here, but know that each and every one of you I appreciate and thank!

Introduction

In today's interconnected world, the digital presence of a business is as vital as the quality of its products or services. While farmers market vendors often thrive on face-to-face interactions and local connections, their success increasingly hinges on their ability to engage customers beyond the market's physical boundaries. Digital branding and social media marketing are not just tools; they are essential components of a modern business strategy. These platforms provide opportunities to reach new audiences, build loyalty among existing customers, and ensure long-term growth and sustainability.

The importance of having a robust digital presence cannot be overstated. Consumers now turn to the internet to discover local businesses, learn about products, and make purchasing decisions. For farmers market vendors, this shift represents both a challenge and an opportunity. A well-executed online strategy allows vendors to showcase their products, tell their stories, and connect with customers before they even step foot in the market. It transforms a business from being just a stall at a market into a recognizable and trusted brand. Without a strong online presence, even the most unique products and experiences risk going unnoticed in today's competitive marketplace.

Farmers market vendors often rely on the community atmosphere of markets to attract customers, but this reliance can create limitations. Social media platforms like Instagram, Facebook, and TikTok empower vendors to extend that sense of community into the digital realm. These platforms are not just for advertising; they are a means to educate, inspire, and connect with customers. Through storytelling, vendors can share the journey of their products—whether it's a farmer growing organic vegetables, an artist crafting handmade jewelry, or a baker preparing fresh loaves of bread. This connection fosters trust and loyalty, making customers more likely to support a vendor not just at the market but also online and beyond.

Understanding your audience is critical in this digital age. Who are your customers, and what are they looking for? Are they health-conscious shoppers seeking organic produce? Are they art enthusiasts searching for unique, handmade items? Identifying and understanding these segments is the foundation of any successful branding or marketing strategy. Social media analytics tools provide insights into customer preferences and behaviors, enabling vendors to tailor their content and offerings to meet these needs. This personalized approach can set vendors apart from competitors who use a one-size-fits-all strategy.

Social media also provides vendors with an unparalleled opportunity to keep their audience engaged and informed. Market-goers want to know what's fresh this week, what special promotions are available, and when their favorite vendors will be at the market. Regular updates, engaging posts, and interactive content—like polls, live videos, and Q&A

sessions—can keep your audience excited and eager to visit. When done consistently and authentically, these efforts create a sense of anticipation and community that extends far beyond the market day.

As you navigate the chapters of this book, you will gain the tools, strategies, and insights needed to build a thriving digital presence for your business. Whether you are a seasoned vendor looking to refine your approach or a newcomer eager to make your mark, this guide will help you harness the power of digital branding and social media marketing. With a clear understanding of your audience, a compelling online presence, and a commitment to engaging your customers, you will be well-equipped to succeed not only in your local market but also in the broader digital marketplace. Your journey to becoming a standout vendor begins here.

Part 1

Foundations of Branding

Chapter 1

Foundations of Branding

Branding is the heart of any successful business. It's more than just a logo or a catchy name; it's the perception your customers have about your business and the promise you deliver with every interaction. For farmers market vendors, branding is especially crucial. It helps you stand out in a vibrant yet competitive environment, build trust with your customers, and turn casual buyers into loyal advocates. A strong brand creates a sense of identity and consistency that resonates with your audience and keeps them coming back.

Building a successful brand requires intention and strategy. It's about understanding your unique value, effectively communicating it, and ensuring that every aspect of your business aligns with your brand's message. For farmers market vendors, a well-crafted brand can transform a simple market stall into a recognizable and trusted name in the community and beyond. Let's explore the foundational elements of branding and how to apply them to your business.

What is Branding?

Branding encompasses the visual, emotional, and experiential elements that define how customers perceive your business. It's about more than just what you sell; it's about how your business makes people feel. A strong brand communicates your values, your mission, and the quality of your products in a way that resonates with your audience. Every interaction, from your logo to your social media posts, contributes to shaping your brand.

For example, consider two vendors selling honey at a farmers market. Vendor A labels their jars as "Local Honey," while Vendor B brands their products as "Golden Harvest: Pure Florida Honey," complete with a vibrant logo featuring a honeybee and a tagline that reads, "Sunshine in Every Drop." Vendor B's branding tells a story and creates an emotional connection, making it far more memorable and appealing to customers.

Branding is what transforms a product from a commodity into a distinctive offering. It's about creating an identity that customers recognize and trust. A well-executed brand can elevate your business, helping you attract more customers and build long-term loyalty.

Defining Your Brand Identity

Your brand identity is the unique combination of elements that represent your business. It's what sets you apart and makes you memorable. To establish a strong brand identity, start by defining your unique selling proposition (USP). What makes your business different from others? Are your products sustainably sourced? Do you use traditional methods or innovative techniques? Highlighting these unique aspects will help you capture customer attention and differentiate your business.

Creating a memorable name, logo, and tagline is another critical step. Your name should be easy to pronounce, spell, and remember. Pair it with a logo that reflects your values and a tagline that communicates your mission. For instance, "Rustic Roots Farm: Fresh Produce, Naturally" tells a story in just a few words. Consistency in your branding elements—colors, fonts, and tone of voice—across all touchpoints reinforces your identity and builds recognition.

Maintaining consistency in your brand identity is crucial. Whether it's your market booth, your packaging, or your online presence, every aspect of your business should align with your brand's message. Consistency builds trust and ensures that your customers know what to expect from your business.

Differentiating Your Brand from Competitors

In a crowded market, standing out requires more than great products. It's about creating an experience that customers can't find anywhere else. Differentiation is essential for capturing attention and building a loyal customer base. Start by emphasizing your authenticity. Share the story behind your business, your values, and your passion. Transparency and authenticity resonate with customers and build trust.

For example, if you're a microgreen grower, you might share videos of your harvesting process on social media or explain how your practices support sustainability. This type of content not only showcases your expertise but also connects with customers on a deeper level. Authenticity fosters loyalty and makes your business more relatable.

Offering a unique experience is another way to stand out. Personalized packaging, free samples, or engaging social media content can make a lasting impression. For instance, a soap maker who includes a handwritten thank-you note with every purchase creates a memorable experience that customers will remember and talk about. Small touches like these can set your business apart from competitors and create a loyal customer base.

The Importance of Branding, Marketing, and Promoting

Consistent branding and marketing are essential for building recognition and driving sales. Customers are more likely to support businesses they recognize and trust. By presenting a cohesive and professional brand image, you make it easier for customers to remember and choose your products.

Marketing and promotion go hand in hand with branding. They ensure that your brand reaches your target audience and stays top of mind. For farmers market vendors, promotion can include social media posts, email newsletters, and in-person interactions. These efforts not only attract new customers but also nurture relationships with existing ones, fostering loyalty and repeat business.

Professionalism is another key aspect of branding and marketing. A well-branded business conveys quality and reliability, which can lead to new opportunities such as partnerships and sponsorships. Over time, these efforts contribute to the long-term success and growth of your business.

Taking Ownership of Your Business Growth

Every vendor must take responsibility for their own branding, marketing, and promotion. While farmers markets provide a platform to sell your products, they cannot market every individual business. It's up to you to create and communicate your brand identity and ensure that your products stand out.

Collaborating with the market can enhance visibility, but it should complement your own efforts. For instance, you can share the market's promotional posts on social media or participate in joint events. However, relying solely on the market's marketing initiatives can limit your growth. By investing in your own marketing materials and strategies, you can reach a broader audience and build a stronger brand.

Taking ownership of your branding and marketing efforts empowers you to shape your business's future. It allows you to control your narrative, connect with your audience, and drive your success. With the right strategies, you can create a brand that stands out and thrives.

The Power of a Great Story: Telling Your "Why"

Stories are a powerful way to connect with customers. Sharing your journey helps customers see the person behind the product and builds a deeper connection. Your story should convey your passion, values, and the mission that drives your business.

For example, a beekeeper might share how their love for pollinators inspired them to start their honey business. An artisan might highlight the traditional techniques they use to create their handmade goods. These stories create an emotional connection that resonates with customers and inspires loyalty.

Telling your story also sets you apart from competitors. It gives customers a reason to choose your products over others. By sharing your "why," you invite customers to become part of your journey. This connection turns buyers into advocates who support your business and share your story with others.

Leveraging Community Engagement

Engaging with your community extends beyond transactions; it's about creating a sense of belonging. Host events at your stall like tasting sessions, educational workshops on sustainable farming, or community meet-ups. These activities can turn your booth into a community hub, increasing visibility and loyalty. For instance, hosting a "Sow and Grow" workshop where customers can learn how to plant their own herb garden using your seeds not only educates them but also builds a community around your brand.

Feedback as a Branding Tool

Use customer feedback as a direct line to improve your branding strategy. Encourage reviews, comments, and direct feedback at the market or through social media platforms. Listening to your customers can reveal what aspects of your branding resonate with them or need adjustment. For example, if customers frequently commend your eco-friendly packaging, you might decide to make it a more prominent part of your brand identity. Conversely, if there's confusion about your product range, you might need to clarify your messaging or product presentation.

Adapting to Market Trends

Staying relevant in a dynamic market like a farmers market means adapting to new trends without losing your brand's core identity. For instance, if there's a growing trend towards organic products, consider how you can authentically integrate this into your branding without compromising your established values. Perhaps you could offer a new line of products or highlight your existing organic offerings more effectively. This adaptability shows your brand is responsive and committed to meeting customer expectations, enhancing trust and engagement.

Closing Thoughts

Branding is more than a business strategy; it's the foundation of how customers perceive and connect with your business. By defining your identity, differentiating yourself from competitors, taking ownership of your growth, and engaging with your community, you'll establish a brand that stands out and thrives. Remember, your story is one of your most powerful tools. Share it authentically, adapt to trends, and use feedback to refine your approach, watching as it transforms your customers into advocates for your brand.

Chapter 2

Visual Branding

Your brand's visual identity is often the first impression customers have of your business. It is what grabs their attention, sparks their interest, and, ideally, keeps your products and services at the forefront of their minds. For farmers market vendors, where customers are often browsing a wide array of stalls and options, effective visual branding can be the key to standing out. In this chapter, we'll delve into the essential elements of visual branding and explore why each component is critical to your success.

Designing a Memorable Logo

Your logo is the cornerstone of your visual brand identity. It's the symbol that customers will associate with your business and products, so it needs to be unique, memorable, and representative of what your business stands for. A well-designed logo sets the tone for your brand and serves as a visual anchor for all your marketing materials.

A great logo should be simple yet impactful. Simplicity ensures that the design is easily recognizable and versatile across various mediums, from business cards to signage and social media. An overly complicated logo may look cluttered and fail to make an impression, especially when scaled down. For example, a farmer selling organic produce might use a clean design featuring a leaf or vegetable to convey freshness and sustainability.

Equally important is ensuring that your logo reflects your brand's values and mission. If you're an artisan who crafts handmade jewelry, your logo might include intricate designs that hint at your craftsmanship and creativity. On the other hand, a food truck operator specializing in bold, spicy flavors might use bright colors and dynamic typography to evoke energy and excitement. Your logo should instantly communicate the essence of your brand to anyone who sees it.

Finally, consider the practical aspects of logo design. Your logo should look great in both color and black-and-white, and it should be adaptable to different sizes and formats. A versatile logo ensures that your branding remains consistent and professional, whether it's printed on product labels, embroidered on aprons, or displayed on your website. Investing in a professionally designed logo can make a significant difference in establishing your business as credible and trustworthy.

Choosing Your Brand Colors and Fonts

Colors and fonts play a crucial role in shaping how your brand is perceived. They evoke emotions, convey messages, and influence customer behavior. Choosing the right color palette and typography is essential for creating a cohesive and appealing visual identity.

Color psychology is a powerful tool in branding. Each color carries specific associations and emotions. For instance, green is often associated with health, nature, and sustainability, making it a popular choice for organic farmers or microgreen growers. Red conveys energy and passion, which could work well for a vendor selling spicy sauces or bold flavors. Blue suggests trust and reliability, ideal for businesses emphasizing consistency and professionalism, such as honey producers or dairy farmers.

In addition to choosing the right colors, consider how they work together. A well-balanced color palette includes primary, secondary, and accent colors that complement each other. These colors should be used consistently across all branding materials, from your logo to your signage and social media posts. Consistency helps customers recognize your brand quickly and reinforces its identity.

Typography is equally important. The fonts you choose should align with your brand's personality and be easy to read. A rustic farm might use serif fonts to convey tradition and authenticity, while a modern food truck might opt for bold, sans-serif fonts to reflect innovation and energy. Using no more than two to three fonts—a primary font for headlines, a secondary font for body text, and an optional accent font for decorative purposes—helps maintain a clean and professional look.

Crafting Consistent Packaging and Displays

Packaging and displays are where your visual branding meets the customer. These elements are not just practical; they're a significant part of your customer's experience. Eye-catching, cohesive packaging and displays can attract attention, convey your brand's story, and enhance the perceived value of your products.

Well-designed packaging is an extension of your brand identity. It should incorporate your logo, colors, and fonts, creating a unified look that customers immediately associate with your business. For example, a soap maker might use eco-friendly materials and earthy tones to emphasize their commitment to sustainability, while a baker specializing in decadent desserts might opt for elegant packaging with rich colors and decorative elements to evoke luxury.

Displays, on the other hand, are your opportunity to make a strong visual impact in person. A neatly arranged and visually appealing booth can draw customers in, while a cluttered or disorganized setup might push them away. Use banners, signage, and tablecloths that feature your brand's colors and logo to create a cohesive and professional appearance. Props and decorations that align with your brand's story—such as wooden crates for a rustic farm or sleek, modern stands for a minimalist brand—can further enhance your display.

The Role of Packaging in Brand Experience

Beyond aesthetics, packaging serves as a direct touchpoint for your brand. Consider how packaging can tell your story or highlight key product features. For instance, a jam producer might use labels that detail the origin of the fruits and the traditional methods used, adding value through storytelling. Transparent packaging for baked goods can showcase the quality and freshness of the product, enhancing consumer trust.

Seasonal and Thematic Visual Adjustments

Adapting your visual branding to seasonal changes or specific themes can keep your brand engaging. For example, during autumn, a cider maker might introduce packaging with fall colors and leaf motifs, aligning with the seasonal mood. This not only refreshes your visual identity but also can attract seasonal shoppers looking for themed products. Similarly, for special events like a local festival, you could create limited edition packaging or booth decorations that tie into the event, making your products more appealing to attendees.

Sustainability in Visual Branding

Sustainability is increasingly influencing consumer choices. Reflecting this in your visual branding can set you apart. Use recyclable or biodegradable materials for packaging; if you're a coffee vendor, for example, switch to compostable cups or bags. Communicate these choices through your design by including symbols or text about eco-friendliness. This not only appeals to environmentally conscious consumers but also positions your brand as forward-thinking and responsible.

Closing Thoughts

Visual branding is a powerful tool for farmers market vendors looking to stand out and succeed. A memorable logo, carefully chosen colors and fonts, and cohesive packaging and displays work together to create a strong and consistent brand identity. These elements not only attract customers but also communicate your values, enhance your credibility, and foster loyalty. By investing in your visual branding, adapting to seasonal themes, and emphasizing sustainability, you're setting the foundation for long-term success and creating a brand that customers will remember and trust.

Chapter 3

Establishing Your Online Home

In today's digital world, having an online presence is no longer optional—it is a necessity for businesses aiming to grow and succeed. While your presence at farmers markets is critical for building relationships and showcasing your products, an online home extends your reach far beyond the local community. Establishing a strong digital foundation allows you to connect with customers, build your brand, and create opportunities for growth. This chapter will explore the key components of establishing your online home: building a website or online store, integrating your brand into digital platforms, setting up a professional email address, and harnessing the power of analytics for growth.

Building a Website or Online Store

A website or online store is the cornerstone of your digital presence. It serves as your business's virtual storefront, providing customers with a central location to learn about your products, explore your brand, and make purchases. In many cases, your website will be the first impression a potential customer has of your business, making it essential to create a professional, user-friendly site.

One of the primary reasons to build a website is to establish credibility. A well-designed site signals that your business is legitimate, professional, and trustworthy. Customers often research businesses online before making a purchase, and not having a website can make your business appear less credible. A simple yet effective website with clear navigation, high-quality images, and concise information about your offerings can significantly enhance your business's reputation.

An online store expands your customer base by allowing those who can't visit the market in person to browse and buy your products from home. Whether selling handmade candles, fresh produce, or baked goods, an e-commerce platform can help generate additional revenue and maintain sales during off-season periods. Platforms like Shopify, Wix, and Squarespace offer user-friendly tools for creating and managing an online store, even for those with minimal technical expertise.

Your website should also serve as a storytelling platform, sharing your brand's journey, posting product updates, and featuring customer testimonials. A blog section can educate customers on your processes, like sustainable farming or craftsmanship. This content not only fosters customer connection but also improves your site's search engine optimization (SEO), helping new customers find your business.

Integrating Your Brand into Digital Platforms

Your website is just one part of your digital identity. Integrating your brand across various platforms ensures consistency and reinforces your brand identity. Social media, email marketing, and online directories are integral to creating a cohesive digital ecosystem.

Social media platforms like Instagram, Facebook, and TikTok are vital for customer engagement and driving traffic to your site. Consistent use of your logo, colors, and tone across these platforms creates a unified experience for your audience. If your website has a rustic aesthetic, mirror that on social media with similar imagery and language to strengthen brand recognition.

Email marketing helps maintain connection with customers, sharing updates, and promoting offers. Ensure your emails match your website's branding for a consistent look. Personalized emails can enhance customer loyalty, like offering birthday discounts or purchase-based recommendations.

Online directories and review platforms like Google My Business and Yelp increase local visibility. Optimizing your listings with your logo and business details, along with managing reviews, builds your online reputation and credibility.

Setting Up a Professional Email Address

A professional email address significantly boosts your business's credibility over generic email services. Using a domain-specific email address like "info@rusticrootsfarm.com (mailto:info@rusticrootsfarm.com)" projects professionalism and organization.

It builds trust, as customers perceive businesses with custom emails as more established. Consistency in branding through email increases recognition. Moreover, using services like Google Workspace or Microsoft 365 allows for multiple email addresses for different departments, aiding in communication management as your business grows. These services also offer better security, protecting against spam and phishing, thus safeguarding your business's reputation.

Utilizing Analytics for Growth

Understanding Analytics:

Analytics involve collecting, analyzing, and interpreting data about your website's and social media's performance. Tools like Google Analytics provide insights into:

- **Traffic Sources:** Where your visitors are coming from (search engines, social media, direct visits). Understanding these sources can help you know where to focus your marketing efforts.
- **User Behavior:** Pages visited, time spent on site, bounce rate (the percentage of visitors who navigate away after viewing only one page). This data shows which content resonates with your audience or where your site might be losing visitors.
- **Conversion Tracking:** How many visitors take desired actions like purchasing or subscribing. This helps in measuring the effectiveness of your site in driving sales or engagement.
- **Demographics:** Information on who your visitors are, including age, gender, location, and interests. Knowing your audience demographics can tailor your marketing and product offerings more effectively.

How to Use Analytics:

Set Up Goals and Conversions:

Define what success looks like for your site (e.g., a sale, a subscription, a contact form submission). Google Analytics allows you to set these as goals to track how effectively your site is meeting these objectives. For instance, if you aim to increase newsletter signups, you can monitor how many visitors complete this action.

Monitor Traffic Patterns:

Understand which pages attract the most traffic and why. If a blog post on "Organic Farming Tips" has high views, it might indicate interest in educational content, suggesting more content in this vein. This can guide your content strategy towards topics that engage your audience.

Analyze User Engagement:

Look at metrics like average session duration and pages per session to gauge how engaging your content is. High bounce rates might suggest your landing pages need improvement in relevance or design. By analyzing this, you can refine your pages to keep visitors longer, potentially leading to higher conversion rates.

Segment Your Audience:

Use demographics to tailor marketing efforts. If analytics show a significant portion of your traffic comes from women aged 25-34, you might focus your content or products towards this demographic. This segmentation can lead to more personalized and effective marketing campaigns.

Examples for Utilizing Analytics:

- **Seasonal Interest:** If you notice that searches for "heirloom tomatoes" spike in June, you could prepare your marketing for that period, perhaps with special promotions or content about tomato varieties. This foresight can optimize your sales during peak interest times.

- **Content Strategy:** Suppose your analytics reveal that your article on "Composting Methods for Home Gardeners" has a high engagement rate. You could expand this into a series, exploring different aspects of sustainable gardening, thereby attracting more visitors interested in this topic. This could involve creating videos, infographics, or interactive webinars.

- **Conversion Optimization:** If data shows that visitors often leave at the checkout stage, you might need to simplify the purchasing process or offer more payment options. Testing different checkout page designs could be informed by where users drop off. A/B testing different layouts or additional payment methods like PayPal or Apple Pay could reduce cart abandonment.

- **Social Media Impact:** If Instagram drives more traffic to your site than other platforms, you might decide to increase your investment in Instagram ads or collaborations with influencers in your niche. This could involve sponsored posts or giveaways that leverage the visual nature of the platform to showcase your products.

Closing Thoughts

Establishing your online home involves more than just having a website; it's about creating an integrated digital strategy where every element from your site to your emails reflects your brand. Utilizing analytics thoroughly allows you to make informed decisions that drive growth, tailor your offerings to meet customer needs, and enhance your market presence. By mastering these digital tools, you not only connect with your current audience but also expand to new customers, ensuring your farmers market business thrives in the digital age.

Part 2

Social Media Basics

Chapter 4

Choosing the Right Platforms

Selecting the right social media platforms for your business is a critical step in building an effective online presence. Each platform offers unique strengths and caters to different types of audiences, making it important to understand which ones align best with your brand and goals. In this chapter, we'll explore some of the most popular platforms and how they can be used to maximize your reach, engagement, and sales.

Facebook: Building Community and Event Promotion

Facebook remains one of the most versatile social media platforms for small businesses. With over 2.9 billion monthly active users, it provides an unparalleled opportunity to connect with your target audience, promote your products, and build a sense of community around your brand.

One of Facebook's greatest strengths is its ability to foster community. Creating a dedicated business page allows you to interact directly with customers, share updates, and answer questions. For example, a honey producer might use their page to share educational posts about bees, host Q&A sessions, or post customer testimonials. This engagement not only strengthens relationships but also encourages word-of-mouth promotion as followers share your content with their networks.

Facebook's event tools are especially valuable for farmers market vendors. You can create event pages for your market appearances, providing details such as location, time, and featured products. This helps customers plan their visits and builds anticipation. For example, a food truck might create an event announcing a special menu item for the week, drawing in customers who are eager to try something new. Furthermore, live videos during events can give followers a real-time feel of the market atmosphere, enhancing engagement.

Facebook Ads and Boosted Posts also offer affordable options for targeted marketing. These tools allow you to reach specific demographics based on location, interests, and behaviors. For instance, a microgreen grower could target health-conscious consumers within a 20-mile radius of their farmers market. With the ability to track engagement and conversions, you can see which types of ads resonate best; perhaps a video ad showing how microgreens are grown performs better than static images. Over time, these insights help refine your advertising strategy to ensure you're getting the best ROI.

Instagram: Visual Storytelling for Products

Instagram is the go-to platform for businesses that rely on visuals to attract and engage customers. With over a billion active users, it's a powerful tool for showcasing your products, sharing behind-the-scenes content, and building an aspirational brand image.

Visual storytelling is at the core of Instagram's appeal. High-quality photos and videos can make your products stand out, whether it's a beautifully arranged display of fresh produce or an artist's intricate craftsmanship. For example, a baker might post a time-lapse video of their bread rising in the oven, giving followers a glimpse into the process that makes their products special. Using Instagram's carousel feature, you can create mini-albums that highlight different aspects of your business, such as your production methods, team members, or customer testimonials.

Instagram Stories and Reels are excellent for engaging with your audience in real-time. Stories disappear after 24 hours, making them perfect for sharing timely updates, flash sales, or "behind-the-scenes" moments. Reels, on the other hand, allow you to create short, engaging videos that showcase your products in action. For example, a candle maker could post a Reel demonstrating how to light and care for their candles, accompanied by calming music and text overlays. Utilizing features like polls or question stickers in Stories can also directly involve your followers, giving them a voice in what content they want to see or what products they're interested in.

Hashtags are another essential feature of Instagram. By using relevant hashtags such as #FarmersMarket, #ShopLocal, or #HandmadeJewelry, you can increase your content's visibility and attract new followers who share your interests. Geotags are equally important, especially for location-based businesses. Tagging your market's location in posts and

Stories makes it easier for local customers to discover your brand. Moreover, partnering with local influencers can amplify your reach, where they might post about your products at the market, tagging your location and business.

TikTok: Short-Form Videos for Engagement

TikTok has revolutionized social media with its focus on short, engaging videos. While it's especially popular among younger audiences, its reach has expanded to include users of all ages and interests. For farmers market vendors, TikTok offers a unique opportunity to showcase creativity, share stories, and connect with customers in an authentic way.

The beauty of TikTok lies in its emphasis on authenticity and entertainment. Unlike platforms that prioritize polished content, TikTok celebrates creativity and spontaneity. A soap maker, for instance, could create a humorous video showing the "life cycle" of a bar of soap, from crafting to customer use. These playful, relatable videos often perform well, gaining traction through likes, shares, and the platform's algorithm.

Trends and challenges are a hallmark of TikTok's culture. Participating in popular trends, such as using trending audio clips or hashtags, can boost your content's visibility and help you reach a broader audience. For example, a farmer might use a trending song to create a "day in the life" video, showing the journey from harvesting crops to setting up at the market. Engaging in challenges like #FarmTok or #FoodieChallenge can also position your brand in front of viewers who are already interested in similar content.

Educational content also thrives on TikTok. Sharing tips, how-to's, and fun facts about your products can position you as an expert in your field. A mushroom grower, for example, could post videos explaining the different varieties they offer and how to cook with them. This type of content not only engages viewers but also drives interest and trust in your brand. You might even collaborate with other niche creators to host educational series, like a week of cooking with mushrooms, enhancing both your reach and credibility.

Pinterest: Inspiration for Niche Products

Pinterest is a visual discovery platform that excels at inspiring users and driving traffic to websites. For businesses offering niche or highly visual products, it can be an incredibly effective tool for reaching customers who are actively searching for ideas and solutions.

One of Pinterest's strengths is its searchability. Users often turn to Pinterest for inspiration, whether they're planning meals, decorating their homes, or finding unique gifts. By creating visually appealing pins that showcase your products, you can position your brand as a go-to resource. For example, a jewelry maker might create boards featuring "Wedding Gift Ideas" or "Boho Accessories," driving traffic to their online store.

Pinterest boards allow you to organize your content in a way that aligns with customer interests. A baker could create boards like "Gluten-Free Treats" or "Seasonal Desserts," each filled with pins linking back to their website or online store. These boards not only attract followers but also establish your brand as a source of inspiration and expertise in your niche. Adding rich pins with detailed product information can further enhance the shopping experience, allowing users to see pricing and availability directly from the pin.

Unlike many other platforms, Pinterest content has a long shelf life. Pins can continue to drive traffic and engagement for months or even years after they're posted. By investing in high-quality, evergreen content, you can create a steady stream of website visitors and potential customers. For instance, a seasonal pin on "Summer Fruit Salads" might continue to attract viewers long after the season has passed, especially if it's paired with a recipe card that encourages users to visit your site for more.

LinkedIn and Twitter: Niche Uses for Networking and Updates

While LinkedIn and Twitter may not be the first platforms that come to mind for farmers market vendors, they offer unique advantages for networking and sharing updates. LinkedIn is particularly useful for B2B connections, while Twitter excels at real-time communication and engagement.

LinkedIn can help you connect with suppliers, local businesses, and industry professionals. A microgreen grower, for example, might use LinkedIn to network with chefs, restaurant owners, or grocery store managers who could become wholesale clients. Sharing posts about your business's achievements, processes, or sustainability practices can position you as a knowledgeable and reliable partner in your industry. Joining or creating groups related to sustainable farming or local food systems can also lead to partnerships or speaking opportunities.

Twitter is ideal for sharing quick updates and engaging in conversations. A food truck operator might use Twitter to post their daily locations, menu updates, or special offers. The platform's real-time nature makes it perfect for announcing last-minute changes, such as weather-related cancellations or new product launches. Engaging with local hashtags or participating in trending topics can also help increase your visibility. For example, tweeting about #FarmersMarket during peak season can attract local users interested in fresh, local produce.

Both platforms are excellent for building credibility and showcasing your expertise. By sharing valuable content, participating in discussions, and connecting with key players in your field, you can enhance your reputation and open doors to new opportunities. For example, a honey producer could share articles about bee conservation or respond to questions from followers, demonstrating their commitment to their craft and community. Regularly engaging with industry influencers or local food bloggers on Twitter can lead to retweets or mentions, further expanding your reach.

Closing Thoughts

Choosing the right social media platforms is essential for maximizing your reach and impact. Each platform offers unique opportunities: from building community and promoting events on Facebook, telling visual stories on Instagram, engaging with short-form videos on TikTok, inspiring through Pinterest, to networking and real-time updates on LinkedIn and Twitter. By understanding each platform's strengths and tailoring your strategy accordingly, you can create a robust online presence that drives growth, builds relationships, and supports your business goals. The key is to be where your audience is, provide value in a way that resonates with them, and use each platform's features to highlight what makes your farmers market business unique.

Chapter 5:
Creating Content That Sells

Content is the lifeblood of your social media strategy. It's what draws people to your page, engages them, and ultimately convinces them to support your business. For farmers market vendors, creating content that effectively showcases your products and tells your story can significantly boost your online presence and sales. In this chapter, we'll discuss the three critical elements of compelling social media content: high-quality photos, engaging videos, and captivating captions.

Photos: High-Quality Visuals for Social Media

Photos are the cornerstone of any visual branding strategy. On platforms like Instagram and Facebook, where visuals dominate, high-quality photos can make your posts stand out and attract attention. As the saying goes, "a picture is worth a thousand words," and in the world of social media, a stunning photo can convey your brand's values, showcase your products, and create an emotional connection with your audience.

Investing in good photography equipment or hiring a professional photographer can make a significant difference. While smartphone cameras are more advanced than ever, lighting, composition, and editing skills are equally important. For example, a soap maker might arrange their products with natural elements like flowers and rustic wood to evoke a sense of craftsmanship and sustainability. Proper lighting, whether natural or artificial, can highlight the textures and details of the soap, making it more appealing to potential customers.

Consistency is also key in creating a recognizable brand aesthetic. Choose a style that aligns with your brand's personality—whether it's bright and cheerful or earthy and minimalist—and stick to it across your posts. Using tools like Lightroom or Canva can help you apply consistent filters and edit your photos to maintain a cohesive look. For instance, if you're selling organic produce, maintain a natural, unfiltered look to emphasize authenticity.

The variety in your photos keeps your audience engaged. Mix product shots with lifestyle photos, such as a customer enjoying your handmade candles or a chef using your microgreens in a dish. Behind-the-scenes photos showing your production process or market setup can also create a sense of authenticity and connection. By diversifying your visuals, you keep your content fresh and interesting while showcasing the many facets of your business. Additionally, consider seasonal themes that resonate with your audience; autumnal setups for fall produce or bright, vibrant colors for summer fruits can align with seasonal shopping trends.

Videos: Showcasing Behind-the-Scenes and Product Features

Videos are a powerful way to bring your products to life and engage your audience on a deeper level. They allow you to demonstrate your products in action, share your story, and connect with viewers in a way that static images cannot. Platforms like TikTok, Instagram Reels, and YouTube are perfect for video content, but even short clips on Facebook can make a big impact.

Behind-the-scenes videos are particularly effective for building trust and transparency. For example, a vegetable farmer might create a video showing the journey from planting seeds to harvesting crops. These videos not only highlight your dedication and effort but also educate customers about the process, making them more likely to appreciate and value your products. Adding text overlays to explain what's happening or share fun facts can enhance viewer engagement.

Demonstration videos are another excellent option. If you're a baker, you could film a step-by-step video showing how to frost cupcakes or create a perfect sourdough loaf. A honey producer might showcase how to pair their honey with cheeses or teas. These videos provide value to your audience, positioning you as an expert in your field while subtly promoting your products. Live demos at the market, captured and shared online, can also drive immediate interest and sales by showing real-time interaction with customers.

Short, engaging clips are ideal for social media platforms with time limits, such as TikTok and Instagram Reels. For example, a mushroom grower could create a quick video featuring different varieties of mushrooms, their unique qualities, and how they're used in cooking. Adding background music and on-screen text can make the content more dynamic and engaging. You might also tap into trending music or dance challenges to make your product videos go viral, like dancing with your market sign or creating a fun, educational challenge around your products.

Finally, don't overlook the importance of storytelling in your videos. Share your brand's mission, introduce your team, or recount a memorable experience at a farmers market. Storytelling creates an emotional connection, turning viewers into loyal customers who feel invested in your success. For example, a video where you interview long-time customers about their favorite products can humanize your brand and foster community.

Captions: Writing Posts That Engage and Convert

Captions are the bridge between your visuals and your audience. A well-crafted caption can provide context, spark engagement, and encourage action. While your photos and videos capture attention, your captions give your audience a reason to stay and interact.

A good caption starts with a hook. The first line should grab the reader's attention and entice them to read more. For example, "Ever wonder how fresh honey makes its way from hive to jar? Let us show you!" or "The secret to the perfect sourdough loaf is simpler than you think!" These hooks create curiosity and invite your audience to engage with your content. Including questions can also prompt interaction, like, "What's your favorite way to enjoy our jams?"

Captions should also reflect your brand's voice. If your brand is friendly and conversational, your captions should feel like a chat with a friend. For example, "Hey, bread lovers! Did you know our sourdough is made with a 100-year-old starter? Come by this Saturday to grab a loaf!" If your brand is more formal, your captions might focus on professionalism and expertise. For instance, "Our handcrafted candles are made with 100% soy wax and infused with natural essential oils for a clean, eco-friendly burn."

Including a call-to-action (CTA) is essential for driving engagement and sales. Encourage your audience to comment, share, or visit your website. Examples include: "Which flavor should we bring to the market next week? Let us know in the comments!" or "Click the link in our bio to pre-order your holiday gift sets today." A strong CTA gives your audience clear instructions on how to interact with your brand.

Here are 10 expanded caption examples to inspire your posts:

1.	Farm-fresh strawberries are here! Sweet, juicy, and picked just for you. 🍓 Which recipe will you try first? Comment below! Visit us this Saturday at the market.

2.	Did you know our bees travel up to 5 miles to collect nectar? 🐝 That's dedication! Taste the difference in every drop of our wildflower honey. Perfect for your tea or toast!

3.	It's soup season! 🥕 Our organic carrots are perfect for hearty, healthy meals. Share your favorite carrot soup recipe in the comments!

4.	Freshly baked and still warm. Our cinnamon rolls are the treat you didn't know you needed. 🥐 Tag someone you'd share this with!

5.	What's your favorite candle scent? 🕯 Lavender, vanilla, or citrus? Let us know below! We'll feature the top choice in our next market setup.

6.	Crafted with love, just for you. Our handmade jewelry makes the perfect gift for someone special (or yourself!). ◆ Click the link in our bio to see our latest collection.

7. Behind every loaf of our bread is a story of tradition, patience, and care. Come taste the difference. What's your favorite bread memory?

8. Our microgreens are packed with flavor and nutrients. Add them to your salads, sandwiches, or smoothies for a healthy boost! Which is your go-to meal with greens?

9. Rain or shine, we're bringing the best of the season to your table. See you Saturday at the farmers market! What weather do you prefer for market days?

10. Our handmade soaps are as gentle on your skin as they are on the planet. Discover your new favorite scent this weekend. Which scent are you most excited about?

Interactive Content and User-Generated Content

Interactive content like polls, quizzes, and Q&A sessions can greatly boost engagement. Instagram Stories, for instance, allow you to ask followers which product they want to see featured next or what they think about a new product idea. This not only engages your audience but also provides valuable feedback for your business decisions.

User-generated content (UGC) is another powerful tool. Encourage your customers to post photos or reviews of your products using a specific hashtag, like #RusticRootsProduce. Featuring these posts on your page not only provides social proof but also fosters a community around your brand. You might even host a contest where customers submit their creative uses of your products, offering prizes like discounts or free samples, which can increase product visibility and customer loyalty.

Closing Thoughts

Creating content that sells is about more than just pretty pictures and clever captions—it's about telling your brand's story, showcasing your products, and connecting with your audience in meaningful ways. High-quality photos capture attention, engaging videos bring your brand to life, and thoughtful captions drive interaction and conversion. By incorporating interactive elements and leveraging user-generated content, you can deepen engagement further. By mastering these elements, you can create a social media presence that not only promotes your business but also builds lasting relationships with your customers, turning casual browsers into loyal supporters.

Chapter 6:

Building an Audience

Building an audience for your business is one of the most crucial steps toward achieving long-term success. For farmers market vendors, this means creating a community of customers who not only love your products but also feel a connection to your brand. However, it's important to understand that building an engaged and loyal audience doesn't happen overnight. It requires consistent effort, strategic actions, and genuine interactions. In this chapter, we will explore how to find and follow your ideal customers, engage with your followers effectively, leverage local community networks to grow your audience, and harness the power of loyalty programs and customer reviews.

Finding and Following Your Ideal Customers

The foundation of building an audience lies in finding and connecting with the right people—your ideal customers. These are individuals who are most likely to value your products and become loyal supporters of your business. Identifying and reaching them requires a deep understanding of your target market.

Start by defining your ideal customer profile. Consider factors such as demographics (age, gender, location, income level), psychographics (values, interests, lifestyle), and behaviors (shopping habits, preferred social media platforms). For example, if you're a microgreen grower, your ideal customers might include health-conscious individuals who prioritize fresh, nutrient-dense foods. On the other hand, if you sell handmade jewelry, your audience might consist of people who appreciate unique, artisan-crafted accessories.

Social media platforms offer powerful tools for finding your ideal customers. Use hashtags related to your niche (e.g., #FarmersMarket, #LocalFood, #HandmadeJewelry) to discover posts and accounts that align with your brand. Follow these accounts and interact with their content to introduce your business to potential customers. For instance, a soap maker could follow accounts focused on eco-friendly living and comment on their posts to build visibility and connections. Additionally, utilize platform features like Instagram's "Explore" or Twitter's "Advanced Search" to find users interested in similar topics.

Collaborations with complementary businesses can also help you reach your target audience. Partner with vendors at your farmers market or other local businesses that share a similar customer base. For example, a honey producer might collaborate with a tea company to create a social media campaign promoting how their products pair perfectly together. This type of partnership not only broadens your reach but also reinforces your brand's credibility by associating it with other trusted businesses. Consider joint Instagram Lives or TikTok challenges where both businesses feature each other's products.

Engaging with Your Followers: Comments, Likes, and Messages

Once you've started attracting followers, the next step is to actively engage with them. Engagement is the key to building relationships, fostering loyalty, and turning casual followers into devoted customers. By consistently interacting with your audience, you demonstrate that your brand values their support and input.

Responding to comments on your posts is one of the simplest yet most effective ways to engage with your followers. When someone takes the time to comment on your content, acknowledge their effort with a thoughtful reply. For example, if a follower compliments your freshly baked bread, you could respond with, "Thank you so much! We'll have even more fresh loaves at this Saturday's market. Hope to see you there!" This type of interaction encourages further dialogue and strengthens the connection. Using emojis or GIFs can add a personal, friendly touch to your responses.

Direct messages (DMs) provide an opportunity for more personal engagement. Use DMs to answer customer inquiries, thank followers for their support, or share exclusive updates. For instance, a candle maker could send a message to loyal customers announcing a new scent and offering them an early-bird discount. Personalized messages make customers feel valued and appreciated, which can lead to increased loyalty and word-of-mouth referrals. You might also use DMs for customer feedback or to resolve any issues privately, showing your commitment to customer satisfaction.

Engaging with your followers' content is just as important as responding to their interactions with your brand. Like and comment on their posts to show genuine interest in their lives and experiences. For example, if a customer shares a photo of your produce in a homemade meal, comment with something like, "That dish looks amazing! We're so glad our veggies could be part of it." This type of interaction fosters a sense of community and encourages customers to share more about their experiences with your brand. Hosting or participating in user-generated content campaigns, like #MyFarmersMarketMeal, can further engage your community.

Leveraging Local Community Networks

Local community networks are a powerful resource for growing your audience. By tapping into these networks, you can connect with customers who value supporting local businesses and establish your brand as an integral part of the community.

Farmers markets themselves are a prime example of a local community network. Building strong relationships with market organizers, fellow vendors, and regular customers can lead to valuable opportunities for collaboration and exposure. For instance, a food truck operator might partner with a local musician to host a special event at the market, attracting new visitors and creating buzz on social media. Regularly sharing updates about your participation in different markets or special events at the market can keep your audience engaged and informed.

Community groups and organizations, both online and offline, are another avenue for audience growth. Join local Facebook groups, Nextdoor communities, or neighborhood forums where your target audience is active. Share relevant updates about your business, such as upcoming market appearances or new product launches, and participate in discussions to establish yourself as a trusted local vendor. For example, a honey producer might join a gardening group and contribute tips on bee-friendly plants, subtly promoting their brand while providing value to the community. Initiating or contributing to community projects, like a local harvest festival, can also enhance your brand's community standing.

Participating in local events beyond the farmers market can also help you reach new customers. Sponsor or participate in events such as school fundraisers, holiday fairs, or community clean-ups. For instance, an artist who creates handmade crafts might set up a booth at a local art walk, showcasing their products to a new audience and building connections with other artists and attendees. These events often have a social media presence where you can gain exposure by tagging the event or using event-specific hashtags.

Lastly, don't underestimate the power of local media. Reach out to newspapers, radio stations, and bloggers who cover community events and small businesses. A feature story about your business—whether it's a profile on your journey or coverage of an upcoming market—can significantly boost your visibility and attract new followers. You might also offer to write guest posts or provide content for local blogs or news sites, like a piece on sustainable farming practices or seasonal recipes using your products.

Loyalty Programs and Customer Reviews

Implementing a loyalty program can be an effective strategy to keep your audience engaged and coming back for more. Offer points, discounts, or exclusive access for repeated purchases or social media engagement. For example, a vendor might offer a "10th Purchase Free" card or special deals for sharing posts about your products. These programs incentivize customers to interact more with your brand, boosting both sales and community feeling.

Encouraging and managing customer reviews is another way to build trust and attract new followers. Positive reviews on platforms like Google, Yelp, or directly on your social media can influence potential customers. After a sale, send a follow-up message asking for feedback or a review, perhaps with a small incentive. Display these reviews on your website or social media; for example, a snapshot of a glowing review on your Instagram story can be very persuasive.

However, handling negative feedback gracefully is equally important. Respond to criticisms with professionalism, offering solutions or apologies where needed. This approach can show future customers that you value all feedback and are committed to improvement, which can enhance your brand's reputation for customer service.

Closing Thoughts

Building an audience takes time, effort, and patience, but the rewards are well worth it. By finding and following your ideal customers, engaging with your followers in meaningful ways, leveraging local community networks, and implementing loyalty programs and encouraging reviews, you can create a loyal and supportive audience that helps your business thrive. Remember, the key is to focus on building genuine relationships and providing value to your audience. With consistent effort and a clear strategy, your audience will grow, and your business will flourish within the community you serve.

Part 3

Advanced Social Media Strategies

Chapter 7:

The Power of Social Proof

Social proof is a powerful psychological principle that influences consumer behavior. When people see others endorsing a product or service, they are more likely to trust and purchase it themselves. For farmers market vendors, leveraging social proof can significantly enhance credibility, attract new customers, and build a loyal following. In this chapter, we will explore how to collect customer reviews, share user-generated content, partner with local influencers, and utilize social media features to maximize the impact of social proof.

Collecting Customer Reviews

Customer reviews are one of the most effective forms of social proof. Positive reviews build trust and reassure potential customers that your products are high-quality and worth purchasing. Encouraging satisfied customers to share their experiences is an essential step in establishing your business as reliable and trustworthy.

Start by making it easy for customers to leave reviews. Include links to your Google My Business, Yelp, or Facebook pages on your receipts, business cards, and website. For example, a honey producer might include a QR code on their product labels that directs customers to a review page. Clear and simple instructions increase the likelihood of customers taking the time to leave feedback. Additionally, consider using in-store or booth signage that prompts reviews, like "Leave Us a Review!" with a link or QR code.

Incentivizing reviews can also be effective. Offer a small discount, free sample, or entry into a giveaway as a thank-you for submitting a review. For instance, a soap maker could run a promotion where customers who leave a review on their website or social media are entered to win a free gift set. This not only encourages reviews but also creates excitement and engagement around your brand. However, ensure that any incentives comply with platform policies to avoid any negative repercussions.

Once you've collected reviews, share them widely to amplify their impact. Post them on your social media pages, feature them on your website, or include them in your marketing materials. For example, a baker could create a visually appealing graphic with a customer's glowing review and pair it with a photo of their best-selling pastries. Highlighting positive feedback not only reinforces trust but also motivates potential customers to make a purchase. You might also consider creating a dedicated "Testimonials" page on your website where all reviews are showcased, making it a central hub for potential customers to see social proof.

Sharing User-Generated Content

User-generated content (UGC) is any content created by your customers that features your products. This can include photos, videos, testimonials, or social media posts. Sharing UGC is an excellent way to showcase your products in real-life settings, build community, and encourage others to engage with your brand.

Encourage customers to share their experiences by creating a branded hashtag. For instance, a microgreen grower might use #FreshWithGreenSprout and invite customers to tag their photos of meals made with their microgreens. This makes it easy to find and share UGC while promoting your brand to a wider audience. You can also run contests or features where the best UGC gets shared or even wins a prize, further incentivizing participation.

When customers post about your products, ask for permission to share their content on your platforms. Most people are flattered to be featured and appreciate the acknowledgment. For example, a candle maker might repost a customer's Instagram story showcasing their candles as part of a cozy evening setup. Sharing this content not only highlights your products but also demonstrates appreciation for your customers. Always credit the original creator, which can lead to further shares and likes from their network.

Sharing UGC also adds authenticity to your marketing. Seeing real people enjoying your products helps potential customers envision themselves doing the same. For instance, a food truck could share a customer's video of their family enjoying a meal, paired with a caption like, "Nothing beats the joy of good food and great company! Thanks for sharing your experience with us, @username!" This type of content is relatable and highly effective in building trust. Additionally, UGC can serve as inspiration for new content strategies or product ideas, providing valuable insights into how your customers use and perceive your products.

Partnering with Local Influencers

Local influencers can play a significant role in boosting your brand's visibility and credibility. Influencers are individuals with a strong following on social media who can promote your products to their audience. Partnering with influencers who align with your brand values can help you reach new customers and enhance your reputation.

Start by identifying influencers in your community who share an interest in your niche. For example, a farmer selling organic produce might connect with a local food blogger or wellness coach, while an artisan jewelry maker might collaborate with a fashion influencer. Look for individuals who have an engaged following rather than focusing solely on follower count; micro-influencers with smaller, highly engaged audiences often deliver better results than larger influencers with lower engagement. Tools like Buzzsumo or local community lists can help you find the right influencers.

When approaching influencers, offer something of value in exchange for their promotion. This could be free products, an exclusive discount for their followers, or a paid partnership. For instance, a baker could provide a box of their best pastries for an influencer to feature in a "weekend brunch" post. Be clear about your expectations, such as the type of content you'd like them to create and the messaging they should use. It's also wise to draft a simple agreement to ensure both parties are clear on deliverables and usage rights.

Collaborate with influencers on creative campaigns that highlight your products in an authentic way. For example, a soap maker could partner with a beauty influencer to create a "self-care routine" video featuring their products. Sharing this content on both the influencer's and your own platforms amplifies its reach and impact. You could also engage in longer-term partnerships, like ongoing product placements or monthly feature posts, to keep your brand top-of-mind.

Track the results of your influencer partnerships to measure their effectiveness. Use metrics like engagement, website traffic, and sales generated from the campaign to determine the return on investment. For example, a honey producer who partners with a local chef might track how many customers used the chef's discount code to purchase their honey. These insights can help you refine your strategy and build more successful collaborations in the future. Consider using UTM parameters or specific promo codes to accurately track the influence of each partnership.

Utilizing Social Media Features for Social Proof

Beyond traditional reviews and UGC, social media platforms offer unique features that can amplify social proof:

- **Instagram Highlights:** Use highlights to keep stories with customer testimonials, product mentions, or influencer collaborations visible long after they disappear from the main story feed.
- **Instagram Reels and TikTok:** Create or encourage content where users can participate in challenges or share their experiences with your products. For example, a "Cooking with [Your Brand]" challenge where users post recipes using your ingredients.

- **Live Sessions:** Host live Q&A sessions, product demos, or live from the farmers market, inviting followers to ask questions or share their thoughts in real-time, fostering an immediate sense of community and trust.
- **Polls and Questions:** Use Instagram Stories or Twitter polls to ask for feedback on products or potential new offerings, showing that you value customer input and are responsive to their needs.
- **Social Media Badges:** Platforms like Twitter allow you to pin your best tweets or retweets that feature positive feedback or UGC, keeping this social proof at the top of your profile for new visitors to see.

Closing Thoughts

Social proof is an invaluable tool for building trust, credibility, and community around your brand. By collecting customer reviews, sharing user-generated content, partnering with local influencers, and leveraging social media features, you can harness the power of social proof to attract new customers and strengthen relationships with existing ones. These strategies not only enhance your online presence but also create a ripple effect that drives long-term success for your business. With consistent effort and a focus on authenticity, social proof can transform your brand into a trusted and beloved part of your community, turning customers into brand ambassadors who actively promote your business.

Chapter 8:

Planning and Scheduling Content

Consistency is the key to success in social media marketing. Without a clear plan, it's easy to fall behind on posting or to produce content that doesn't align with your brand's goals. Planning and scheduling your content in advance allows you to maintain a steady presence online, stay relevant, and maximize your audience's engagement. In this chapter, we will explore how to create a content calendar, the tools available for scheduling posts, how to align your content with seasons and events for maximum impact, and strategies for dealing with spontaneous content opportunities.

Creating a Content Calendar

A content calendar is a strategic tool that helps you plan, organize, and visualize your social media content over a specific period. It provides structure, ensures consistency, and allows you to align your posts with your business goals and audience interests.

To create a content calendar, start by determining your posting frequency. How often can you realistically post while maintaining quality? For example, a microgreen grower might commit to posting three times a week: one educational post about microgreens, one behind-the-scenes look at the growing process, and one promotional post highlighting a market appearance. It's crucial to balance frequency with quality to avoid overwhelming your followers or diluting your brand message.

Next, decide on the types of content you want to include. Mix educational posts, product showcases, behind-the-scenes content, user-generated content, and promotional announcements. For instance, a soap maker might plan a monthly schedule with themes such as "Ingredient Spotlight Mondays," "Testimonial Thursdays," and "Weekend Sale Announcements." This variety keeps your audience engaged and ensures your posts serve multiple purposes. Including a mix of evergreen content (which remains relevant over time) with timely posts can help maintain interest throughout the year.

Once you've established your content types and frequency, map them out on a calendar. Use tools like Google Calendar, Excel spreadsheets, or specialized content planning platforms like Trello or Asana. Include details for each post, such as the caption, hashtags, images, and intended platform. For example, a farmer might schedule a post for the first Friday of the month featuring a recipe using their seasonal produce, accompanied by a photo and the hashtags #FarmToTable and

#EatSeasonal. Adding notes on the purpose of each post or the target demographic can further refine your strategy.

Tools for Scheduling Posts

Scheduling tools streamline the process of posting content and ensure that your audience sees your posts at optimal times, even if you're busy or unavailable. There are many tools available to help you automate your social media posting, each with its unique features and benefits.

One popular option is Meta Business Suite, which allows you to schedule posts for Facebook and Instagram. This free tool provides an easy-to-use interface where you can upload your content, preview posts, and select publishing times. For example, a food truck might use Meta Business Suite to schedule a week's worth of posts announcing their daily locations and featured menu items. Additionally, features like Instagram Stories scheduling can be particularly useful for daily updates.

For multi-platform management, tools like Buffer, Hootsuite, or Later are excellent choices. These platforms enable you to schedule posts for various social media channels, monitor engagement, and analyze performance metrics. A jewelry maker, for instance, could use Hootsuite to schedule posts for Instagram, Pinterest, and Twitter, ensuring their audience stays engaged across platforms. These tools often include features like hashtag suggestions or optimal posting times based on your audience's behavior.

Advanced tools like Sprout Social or CoSchedule offer additional features such as content performance analytics, collaboration workflows, and the ability to reschedule top-performing posts. These tools are particularly useful for businesses with larger audiences or teams managing multiple accounts. For example, a honey producer could use Sprout Social to track which types of posts generate the most sales and adjust their strategy accordingly. They also provide insights into audience demographics, helping tailor content more precisely.

Many scheduling tools also include features for optimizing post timing. By analyzing when your audience is most active, these tools help you publish content at times when it's likely to receive the most engagement. For example, an artisan baker might discover through Buffer analytics that their audience is most active at 9 AM and 7 PM, allowing them to schedule posts during those windows for maximum visibility. This data-driven approach ensures your content gets seen by the majority of your followers.

Aligning Your Posts with Seasons and Events

Seasonality and events provide excellent opportunities to create relevant and engaging content. Aligning your posts with holidays, seasons, and community events not only keeps your content fresh but also helps you connect with your audience on a deeper level.

Seasonal content is particularly effective for farmers market vendors. For example, a vegetable farmer might create posts showcasing fall recipes using pumpkins or squash, accompanied by captions like, "Nothing says autumn like homemade pumpkin soup! Find everything you need at this Saturday's market." Seasonal content demonstrates that your business is in tune with your customers' needs and interests. Planning a content series around seasonal produce, like "Summer Fruit Series" or "Winter Root Vegetables," can keep your feed relevant and engaging.

Holidays are another excellent source of inspiration. For instance, a candle maker could run a Valentine's Day campaign featuring gift sets, with posts like, "Show your loved ones how much you care with the perfect candle gift set. Order now to make Valentine's Day extra special!" Aligning your posts with holidays helps you tap into the excitement and spending habits surrounding these occasions. Consider creating holiday-specific promotions or themed content, like Easter egg decorating with natural dyes or a Christmas market special.

Community events, such as local festivals or farmers markets, are also worth highlighting in your content. A food truck operator might create posts counting down to a popular local event, sharing sneak peeks of their special event menu. This not only builds anticipation but also encourages your followers to attend. Participating in event hashtags or collaborating with event organizers for cross-promotion can significantly increase your visibility.

Don't forget to plan content around your own business milestones. Celebrate anniversaries, product launches, or reaching a certain number of followers with special posts. For example, an artisan crafter could share a post thanking their followers for helping them reach 1,000 Instagram followers, coupled with a giveaway to celebrate the milestone. This not only boosts engagement but also fosters a sense of community and loyalty among your followers.

Dealing with Spontaneous Content Opportunities

While planning is key, the dynamic nature of social media means there will be times when spontaneous content opportunities arise. These could be in response to real-time events, customer feedback, or trending topics relevant to your brand.

- **Real-Time Engagement:** If there's a sudden weather change affecting your market day, a quick post can inform your followers. For example, "Rain or shine, we're at the market! Come grab some comfort food to warm up today."
- **Trending Topics:** Jump on trends when they align with your brand. If there's a viral challenge or hashtag that fits your niche,

like #GardenChallenge, engage with it by posting your unique take, perhaps showing how your products can be used in gardening.

- **Customer Interaction:** If a customer posts about loving your product, repost or reshare with a comment. This not only amplifies positive feedback but also shows responsiveness, e.g., "Thanks for the love, @customername! Your homemade jam looks delicious!"

Planning for spontaneity in your content calendar by leaving some slots open for last-minute posts can ensure you remain agile. Tools like Buffer allow for easy, quick scheduling even for immediate posts, blending the benefits of planning with the flexibility to react quickly to real-world events.

Closing Thoughts

Planning and scheduling your content is an essential part of maintaining a consistent and effective social media presence. By creating a content calendar, utilizing scheduling tools, aligning your posts with seasons and events, and being ready for spontaneous content opportunities, you can streamline your efforts and maximize your impact. These strategies not only save time but also ensure that your content resonates with your audience and keeps your brand at the forefront of their minds. With careful planning and execution, your social media strategy can become a powerful driver of growth and success for your business.

Chapter 9:

Paid Advertising on a Budget

Paid advertising can be a game-changer for small businesses, especially for farmers market vendors looking to expand their reach and drive sales. The key to success lies in making the most of your budget by targeting the right audience and measuring your results effectively. In this chapter, we'll explore strategies for running Facebook and Instagram ads, boosting posts to increase visibility, analyzing the return on investment (ROI) to optimize your campaigns, and exploring additional cost-effective advertising options.

Running Facebook and Instagram Ads

Facebook and Instagram ads are powerful tools for reaching your target audience. These platforms allow you to create highly targeted campaigns based on demographics, interests, behaviors, and even location. For small businesses, this precision targeting ensures that every dollar spent is reaching the most relevant audience.

To get started, identify your campaign goal. Are you looking to drive traffic to your website, increase sales, or grow your social media following? For example, a honey producer might run an ad campaign to promote a new flavor of honey, directing viewers to their online store. Clearly defining your goal helps you tailor your ad content and targeting strategy. Consider setting up A/B tests where you vary elements like headlines or images to see what resonates best with your audience.

When creating your ad, focus on compelling visuals and clear messaging. A vegetable farmer could use a vibrant photo of their freshest produce with a headline like, "Locally Grown, Freshly Picked: Available at Saturday's Market!" Pair this with a call-to-action (CTA) such as "Learn More" or "Shop Now" to guide viewers toward your desired outcome. Short, engaging videos can also be highly effective, particularly on Instagram, where video content tends to perform better. For instance, a video showing the journey from farm to market can create a compelling narrative that connects with consumers.

Budgeting is a critical aspect of running Facebook and Instagram ads. Start small, with a daily budget of $5-$10, and monitor your results. Use Facebook's Ad Manager or Instagram's Promote feature to adjust your targeting and content based on performance. For instance, if you notice higher engagement from users in a specific location, consider narrowing your geographic targeting to maximize ROI. Use the platform's lookalike audiences feature to find new customers who are similar to your best existing ones, thereby increasing the efficiency of your ad spend.

Boosting Posts for Increased Visibility

Boosting posts is a simpler and more budget-friendly way to reach a broader audience without creating a full ad campaign. This option allows you to amplify the reach of your existing posts by targeting specific demographics and interests.

To boost a post effectively, choose content that has already performed well organically. For example, if a candle maker's post about their new lavender-scented candles received high engagement, boosting it can help it reach even more potential customers. Select a clear goal for the boosted post, such as driving traffic to your website or increasing event attendance.

Targeting is key when boosting posts. Platforms like Facebook and Instagram allow you to specify your audience based on age, location, gender, and interests. For instance, a baker promoting a new line of gluten-free pastries might target health-conscious individuals within a 20-mile radius of their farmers market. This ensures that your boosted post reaches people who are most likely to be interested in your product. You can also target based on behaviors, like people who have shown interest in similar products or local events.

Set a budget and duration for your boost. A small budget of $20 over three days can yield significant results if your targeting is precise. Monitor the performance of the boosted post using insights provided by the platform. Metrics such as reach, engagement, and clicks can help you determine whether the boost was successful and inform your future strategies. Remember, boosting can be particularly effective for time-sensitive promotions like flash sales or special market days.

Analyzing ROI for Small Budgets

Analyzing the return on investment (ROI) of your paid advertising efforts is essential for making informed decisions and optimizing your budget. ROI measures the revenue generated from your ads compared to the amount spent, helping you understand the effectiveness of your campaigns.

Start by tracking key metrics such as clicks, conversions, and sales. For example, if a food truck operator runs a $50 ad campaign promoting their weekly specials, they should track how many customers mention the ad or use a specific discount code included in the campaign. This provides a direct way to measure the campaign's impact on sales. Use Google Analytics or similar tools to track website behavior after ad exposure, such as time spent on site or pages visited.

Use analytics tools provided by platforms like Facebook and Instagram to gain deeper insights into your ad performance. These tools can show you which ads are generating the most engagement, which demographics are responding best, and how much you're paying per click or conversion. For instance, a soap maker might discover that ads targeting eco-conscious women aged 25-40 are driving the most sales, prompting them to focus future campaigns on this audience. Look at metrics like cost per action (CPA) to see if your ad spend is cost-effective.

Adjust your strategy based on the data. If a particular type of ad isn't performing well, experiment with different visuals, headlines, or CTAs. For example, a jewelry maker who finds that video ads are outperforming static images might allocate more of their budget to video content in future campaigns. Small adjustments can lead to significant improvements in ROI over time. Also, consider the lifetime value of a customer; an ad might have a high initial cost but could be worth it if it brings in repeat customers.

Finally, keep your goals realistic and celebrate incremental successes. Paid advertising on a budget is about steady growth rather than overnight results. By consistently analyzing and refining your approach, you can maximize the impact of your spending and achieve sustainable success for your business.

Exploring Additional Cost-Effective Advertising Options

While focusing on social media ads, it's also wise to consider other cost-effective advertising avenues:

- **Google Ads for Local Searches:** Use Google Ads to target people searching for local products or services. Even with a small budget, you can bid on keywords like "farmers market near me" or "local honey." Google's location targeting ensures your ads appear to users in your area.

- **Community Boards and Local Newsletters:** Many communities have digital or physical boards for local advertisements. Sponsoring or placing ads in local newsletters or community apps like Nextdoor can be very cost-effective and reach a highly relevant audience.

- **Pinterest Ads:** If your products are visually appealing, consider Pinterest ads. They allow you to target based on interests and can drive traffic to your online store or blog. For example, a farmer could promote a pin linking to a blog post about seasonal recipes with their produce.

- **Influencer Micro-Partnerships:** Instead of large influencer campaigns, micro-partnerships with local influencers can be budget-friendly. They might post about your products or events in exchange for samples or small fees, offering a personal touch to your advertising.

- **Retargeting Campaigns:** Use retargeting to bring back visitors who didn't convert on their first visit. This method is often more cost-effective since you're targeting an audience already familiar with your brand.

Closing Thoughts

Paid advertising is a valuable tool for farmers market vendors looking to expand their reach and grow their customer base. By running targeted Facebook and Instagram ads, boosting high-performing posts, analyzing ROI, and exploring additional cost-effective advertising methods, you can make the most of your budget and achieve measurable results. Remember, the key to success is experimentation, monitoring, and continuous improvement. With time and effort, even a small advertising budget can yield significant returns for your business, helping you to turn occasional market-goers into loyal customers.

Part 4

Engaging Your Community

Chapter 10:

Social Media and Farmers Markets

Social media is a powerful tool for promoting farmers markets and connecting with customers. For vendors, these platforms offer opportunities to showcase their products, foster community engagement, and increase attendance at market events. In this chapter, we'll explore three key strategies: promoting market dates and locations, cross-promoting with other vendors, highlighting your market's unique atmosphere, and additional tactics like leveraging live events and using social media for market feedback.

Promoting Market Dates and Locations

One of the primary uses of social media for farmers market vendors is to inform and remind customers about market dates and locations. Consistent promotion ensures that your audience knows when and where they can find your products, reducing the chances of missed opportunities.

Start by creating a weekly post template that includes essential information such as the market's name, address, hours, and any special notes like parking details or live entertainment. For example, a honey producer might post, "Find us this Saturday at the Downtown Farmers Market, 9 AM - 1 PM, at Main Street Park! Come for the honey, stay for the live music and local eats. 🎵 " Adding engaging visuals, such as photos of your booth or products, can make these posts more eye-catching and shareable. Use consistent branding elements like your logo or a specific color scheme to enhance recognition.

Incorporate countdowns and reminders into your posting schedule. A vegetable farmer could share a midweek post saying, "Only 3 days until market day! We're bringing fresh-picked heirloom tomatoes, cucumbers, and more. Don't miss out!" On the day before the market, a final reminder post could include specific highlights, such as special discounts or featured items. Using countdown stickers in Instagram Stories can create a sense of urgency and anticipation.

Leverage Instagram and Facebook Stories for real-time updates about your market attendance. These temporary posts are perfect for sharing quick reminders, such as, "We're all set up at the market! Stop by Booth #12 to grab your fresh flowers." Stories allow for immediate engagement and keep your audience informed, especially for last-minute announcements. You might also use polls or question stickers in Stories to ask followers what they're most excited to see or buy, enhancing interaction.

Engage with local hashtags and geotags to amplify your reach. Adding tags like #LocalFarmersMarket or geotags for your market's location can attract new customers searching for local events. For example, a food truck operator might post, "Find us at the City Market this weekend! #StreetFoodLovers #FarmersMarketFun." These strategies ensure your posts reach beyond your existing followers to potential new customers. Participating in Instagram's "Explore" page by using popular local hashtags can also help your content appear to users interested in similar content.

Cross-Promoting with Other Vendors

Collaboration with fellow vendors can significantly boost your visibility and foster a sense of community. Cross-promoting allows you to tap into each other's audiences, attracting new customers who share similar interests.

Start by building relationships with vendors whose products complement your own. For instance, a bread baker could partner with a jam maker to create a joint post featuring "Perfect Pairings" for market-goers. The post might say, "Nothing beats fresh bread with artisanal jam! Find us side by side at this Saturday's Farmers Market." Cross-promotion not only benefits both businesses but also offers added value to your shared audience. Hosting a live session together on Instagram or doing a joint TikTok challenge can further engage both audiences.

Highlight other vendors in your social media posts and Stories. For example, a microgreen grower might share a Story saying, "Shoutout to @LocalCheeseShop their cheese pairs perfectly with our arugula microgreens! Grab both at the market this Sunday." These shoutouts create goodwill among vendors and introduce your audience to new products they may love. Tagging vendors in your posts or Stories can lead to reciprocal promotions, expanding your network.

Collaborate on giveaways to drive engagement and expand your reach. A soap maker and a candle maker might team up to offer a "Relaxation Bundle" as a prize. The giveaway rules could require participants to follow both vendors, like the post, and tag a friend. This strategy increases visibility for both businesses while building excitement for the market. Consider themed giveaways around market events or holidays, like a "Summer BBQ Kit" with contributions from multiple vendors.

Consider creating joint content that tells a story. For example, a mushroom grower and a local chef could collaborate on a cooking video featuring fresh mushrooms. The video could be shared across both accounts, showcasing the mushrooms' versatility and driving traffic to both businesses at the market. This content can be repurposed for blog posts or newsletters, extending its reach.

Finally, engage with other vendors' content by liking, commenting, and sharing their posts. For example, if a coffee vendor posts about their new cold brew, a bread baker might comment, "Can't wait to pair this with our fresh sourdough at Saturday's market!" These interactions foster collaboration and increase your visibility across the market's community. Building a supportive network where vendors regularly interact with each other's content can lead to a more vibrant market atmosphere.

Highlighting Your Market's Unique Atmosphere

Farmers markets are about more than just shopping; they're vibrant community events that offer unique experiences. Highlighting the atmosphere of your market in your social media content helps attract visitors and creates excitement about attending.

Capture the sights, sounds, and energy of the market through photos and videos. For example, a food truck operator could post a video showing the hustle and bustle of the market, accompanied by the caption, "The best vibes, the best food, and the best people—all in one place. Come see us this Sunday at the Farmers Market!" Including details about live music, family-friendly activities, or special events adds to the appeal. Use background music in videos to set the mood, but ensure you have the rights to the music or use royalty-free tracks.

Spotlight the diversity of vendors to showcase the market's variety. For instance, a vegetable farmer might share a post featuring their booth alongside those of an artisan bread maker and a handcrafted soap vendor. The caption could read, "From farm-fresh veggies to handmade goods, there's something for everyone at the Downtown Farmers Market." Highlighting the market's wide array of offerings encourages people to attend and explore. Consider creating a "Meet the Vendors" series where each week you feature a different vendor, sharing their story and products.

Customer stories and testimonials also bring the market's atmosphere to life. Share photos of happy customers enjoying your products, and include quotes or anecdotes about their experience. For example, a honey producer might post, "'This is the best honey I've ever tasted!' Thank you, Sarah, for stopping by and sharing your love for local honey. See you next week!" These personal touches create an emotional connection with your audience. Encourage customers to share their own stories or photos using your market's hashtag.

Seasonal themes and decorations can also enhance your content. For example, during the fall, a baker might post a photo of their pumpkin muffins displayed alongside festive pumpkins and leaves, captioned, "It's fall, y'all! Come grab a taste of the season at this Saturday's market." Aligning your posts with the market's seasonal atmosphere creates a sense of timeliness and excitement. Engage with seasonal trends by creating content around holidays or local harvest festivals.

Leveraging Live Events and Feedback

- **Live Events:** Use platforms like Instagram Live or TikTok Live to broadcast from the market. This could be a live cooking demo using market ingredients, a tour of your booth, or even a Q&A session with customers. For instance, a jewelry maker might do a live session showing how they craft their pieces, inviting questions from viewers. Live events can create real-time engagement and give followers a feel of the market's vibe.

- **Feedback and Interaction:** Social media is not just for broadcasting; it's for interaction. Use polls, questions, or feedback forms to gather input from your audience. For example, ask followers what new products they'd like to see at the market or what they thought of last week's event. This not only provides valuable insights but also makes your followers feel heard and involved.

- **Market Feedback:** After market days, share recaps or highlights, asking for feedback on what could make the experience better. Posting summaries like, "What a fantastic day at the market! What was your highlight? Let us know in the comments!" can spur engagement and provide useful data for future market planning.

Closing Thoughts

Social media offers countless opportunities for farmers market vendors to promote their presence, collaborate with others, highlight the unique atmosphere of their markets, and engage with the community through live events and feedback. By consistently sharing information about market dates and locations, cross-promoting with fellow vendors, capturing the energy of the market, and actively seeking and responding to customer input, you can attract more visitors and foster a loyal customer base. These strategies not only help your business thrive but also contribute to the success and growth of the entire market community. Remember, the key is to build relationships, tell stories, and make every follower feel like part of the vibrant market experience.

Chapter 11:

Collaborating with Others

Collaboration is a powerful way to expand your reach, build relationships, and grow your presence at farmers markets and beyond. Working with others allows you to tap into new audiences, enhance your brand's visibility, and create a sense of community that benefits all parties involved. In this chapter, we will delve into strategies for co-hosting giveaways, partnering with nearby small businesses, networking with local organizations and influencers, balancing collaboration with individual responsibility, and exploring new avenues like joint product development.

Co-hosting Giveaways

Giveaways are an excellent way to boost engagement, attract new followers, and reward loyal customers. Co-hosting a giveaway with other vendors amplifies the impact by combining audiences and creating a more enticing prize package. The key to a successful giveaway lies in strategic planning and clear communication.

When organizing a co-hosted giveaway, choose partners whose products or services complement yours. For example, a bread baker might collaborate with a jam maker and a tea vendor to offer a "Breakfast Basket" giveaway. The combination of items provides added value to participants and highlights each vendor's offerings. Consider seasonal themes or special occasions like holidays to make the giveaway even more appealing, such as a "Holiday Baking Kit" during Christmas.

Set clear rules and expectations for the giveaway. Outline how participants can enter, such as following all collaborating vendors on social media, liking the giveaway post, and tagging friends in the comments. For example, a post might say, "Win the ultimate breakfast basket! Follow @BreadCo, @JamDelights, and @TeaTime, like this post, and tag a friend. Each tag counts as an entry!" Clearly state the deadline for entries and when the winner will be announced. Use tools like Gleam or Rafflecopter for easier management of entries and selection of winners.

Promote the giveaway consistently across all collaborators' platforms. Share engaging visuals of the prize package and encourage each vendor to highlight their contribution. For instance, the tea vendor might post a photo of their tea alongside fresh bread and jam, captioned, "The perfect start to your morning could be yours! Enter now to win this amazing giveaway." Cross-promotion ensures maximum visibility and participation. Use Stories and Reels for countdowns or sneak peeks, adding urgency and excitement.

Once the winner is announced, follow up by thanking participants and promoting your next appearance at the market. Highlight the collaborative aspect of the giveaway to reinforce the sense of community among vendors and customers. For example, "A big thank you to everyone who entered our Breakfast Basket giveaway! Congratulations to @LuckyWinner. Find us all at this Saturday's Farmers Market to stock up on your favorites." Sharing testimonials or photos from the winner can further engage your community.

Partnering with Nearby Small Businesses

Partnering with nearby small businesses offers opportunities to cross-promote and reach new audiences. Collaborations with businesses outside the market can introduce your brand to customers who may not yet be familiar with your products.

Identify businesses that align with your brand's values and audience. For example, a vegetable farmer might partner with a local health food store to offer bundled deals, such as a "Farm-to-Table Box" containing fresh produce and complementary pantry staples. These partnerships highlight your shared commitment to quality and sustainability. Consider joint membership programs where purchases at one business can earn points or discounts at the other.

Co-hosting events or workshops is another way to collaborate with local businesses. For instance, a honey producer could team up with a yoga studio to host a "Sweet Wellness" workshop featuring a yoga session followed by a honey-tasting experience. This type of event attracts participants from both businesses' customer bases, creating a win-win scenario. You might also organize cooking classes, where local chefs use your products to create dishes, thereby promoting both your produce and their culinary skills.

Collaborations can also extend to online promotions. Partner with a local boutique or café to run a social media campaign featuring both brands. For example, a soap maker might work with a boutique to create a "Self-Care Bundle" giveaway. Each partner promotes the campaign to their followers, increasing visibility for both businesses. Consider using interactive features like Instagram's "Swipe Up" or link in bio to direct traffic to each other's sites or special promotional pages.

Track the results of your partnerships to assess their effectiveness. Monitor engagement, sales, and customer feedback to determine the impact of the collaboration. For instance, if a bakery's partnership with a local coffee shop leads to increased foot traffic at the market, it's a clear indicator of success. Use tools like Google Analytics to track website visits or unique codes for sales tracking.

Networking with Local Organizations and Influencers

Building relationships with local organizations and influencers can greatly enhance your brand's visibility and reputation. These partnerships connect you with established networks and trusted voices within your community.

Start by identifying organizations that align with your mission. For example, a mushroom grower might collaborate with a local environmental nonprofit to promote sustainable farming practices. Participating in their events, such as eco-fairs or educational workshops, provides exposure to an audience that values your commitment to sustainability. You could offer to speak at these events or sponsor activities, further embedding your brand within the community.

Local influencers can amplify your reach by sharing your products with their followers. Choose influencers whose audience aligns with your target market. For instance, a jewelry maker might partner with a fashion influencer known for highlighting handmade and unique accessories. Offer them free samples or a discount in exchange for an honest review or social media post. Going beyond just product placement, involve influencers in your brand's narrative, like sharing a day in the life at the market or the process behind your products.

Create authentic partnerships with influencers by involving them in your brand's story. For example, invite a food blogger to visit your booth at the market and document their experience. A post like, "Loved chatting with @LocalFoodie about our seasonal produce! Check out their Stories for a behind-the-scenes look at our farm-to-market journey," creates buzz and builds credibility. Hosting an influencer for a day can also lead to content like blogs, YouTube videos, or Instagram Reels, which have a longer shelf life.

Measure the impact of your networking efforts by tracking metrics such as website traffic, social media engagement, and sales. Adjust your strategy based on what resonates most with your audience. For instance, if an influencer's post leads to a surge in market attendance, consider developing an ongoing partnership. Regularity in collaboration can turn one-time promotions into sustained visibility.

Joint Product Development

Another avenue for collaboration is through joint product development. This involves working with other vendors or local artisans to create unique offerings that neither could produce alone:

- **Product Innovation:** A farmer selling herbs might collaborate with a local distillery to create herbal spirits or flavored vinegar.

This not only introduces new products but can also lead to shared marketing campaigns around the launch.

- **Limited Edition Items:** Craft a limited edition product for special occasions like local festivals or market anniversaries. For example, a cheese maker and a winemaker could produce a "Harvest Pair" for the fall season.

- **Bundled Offerings:** Combine your products with another vendor's to offer themed bundles. A soap maker and a candle maker might offer a "Spa Day" set, enhancing the appeal and perceived value of each product when sold together.

- **Educational Content:** Develop content or kits that educate consumers on how to use or cook with your combined products. For instance, a herb grower and a spice vendor could create a "Flavor Fusion" kit with recipes and ingredients.

Balancing Collaboration with Individual Responsibility

While collaboration is invaluable, it's essential to balance joint efforts with individual responsibility for your branding and marketing. Farmers markets provide a platform for visibility, but each vendor must actively promote their own business.

Understand the role of the farmers market in marketing via the event as a whole. Markets typically focus on attracting visitors to the venue, highlighting the variety of vendors, and promoting the overall experience. However, they cannot effectively market every individual business. For example, a market may advertise live music and fresh produce but leave it to vendors to spotlight their specific offerings.

Align your branding efforts with the market's promotions. Use the market's hashtags, share their posts, and mention their events in your content. For instance, a food truck operator might post, "We're thrilled to be part of the City Farmers Market this weekend! Stop by for your favorite street eats and more. #CityFarmersMarket." This strategy leverages the market's reach while maintaining your unique voice.

Create independent content that complements the market's advertising. For example, a soap maker might share a video showing their production process, captioned, "See how our handmade soaps come to life! Find us this Saturday at Booth 14 at the Downtown Farmers Market." This approach keeps your audience engaged without relying solely on market-wide promotions. Regularly post about your unique selling points, special offerings, or customer testimonials to maintain your individual brand identity.

Closing Thoughts

Collaboration is a cornerstone of success for farmers market vendors. By co-hosting giveaways, partnering with local businesses, networking with organizations and influencers, exploring joint product development, and balancing collaboration with individual responsibility, you can amplify your reach and build lasting connections. Aligning your branding efforts with the market's promotions and actively engaging in collaborative initiatives ensures that your business thrives in a competitive environment while contributing to the market's overall success. Remember, the synergy between individual initiative and community collaboration can lead to both personal growth and collective prosperity.

Chapter 12:

Handling Customer Inquiries and Feedback

Customer inquiries and feedback are invaluable for understanding your audience, building trust, and improving your business. Whether it's a comment on a social media post, a direct message, or a review, how you respond shapes the customer's perception of your brand. In this chapter, we'll delve into strategies for responding promptly to comments and messages, managing negative feedback effectively, leveraging feedback to enhance your offerings and customer experience, and exploring advanced methods to engage and learn from your audience.

Responding to Comments and Messages Promptly

Timely responses to customer comments and messages show that you value their input and care about their experience. Prompt communication fosters trust and builds a positive relationship with your audience. In the fast-paced digital world, delays in responses can lead to missed opportunities and diminished customer satisfaction.

Make it a priority to check your social media platforms and email regularly. Set aside specific times each day to review and respond to inquiries. For example, a food truck vendor might allocate 30 minutes in the morning and evening to address questions about their menu or locations. This consistent engagement ensures that no inquiry goes unanswered. Use scheduling tools or reminders to maintain this routine, especially during busy market seasons.

Use personalized responses to create a stronger connection with your customers. Instead of generic replies, address the customer by name and acknowledge their specific comment or question. For instance, if a customer asks about the availability of your artisan soaps, you might respond with, "Hi Sarah! Thank you for reaching out. We'll have our lavender and oatmeal soaps at this Saturday's market. We'd love for you to stop by!" This approach makes customers feel seen and appreciated. If you handle a high volume of inquiries, consider using templates but personalize them by inserting the customer's name and specific details.

For frequently asked questions, consider creating a dedicated FAQ section on your website or a highlight reel on Instagram. This can include details about product availability, pricing, shipping, and market locations. Directing customers to these resources saves time while still addressing their needs. For example, a vegetable farmer could create an Instagram Story Highlight titled "Market FAQs" with answers to common questions about their produce. Regularly update this section based on new inquiries to keep it relevant.

Finally, use automation tools judiciously. Platforms like Facebook Messenger and Instagram offer features to set up automated responses for common inquiries. For instance, an automated message could say, "Thank you for your message! We'll get back to you within 24 hours. In the meantime, check out our FAQ section for quick answers." While automation can be helpful, ensure that it doesn't replace personalized engagement entirely. Set up notifications for when a customer responds to an automated message to continue the conversation personally.

Managing Negative Feedback

Negative feedback is an inevitable part of running a business, but how you handle it can make or break your reputation. Addressing complaints with professionalism and empathy demonstrates your commitment to customer satisfaction and can turn dissatisfied customers into loyal advocates.

The first step in managing negative feedback is to remain calm and avoid responding defensively. Take a moment to understand the customer's perspective and acknowledge their concerns. For example, if a customer leaves a review stating that your candles arrived damaged, you might respond with, "We're so sorry to hear about this experience. We take great care in packaging our products, but it seems something went wrong this time. Let us make it right for you." This approach validates their feelings and shows a willingness to resolve the issue.

Offer a solution that aligns with the customer's expectations. Whether it's a refund, replacement, or discount on a future purchase, your response should demonstrate that you value their business. For instance, a honey producer might say, "We'd be happy to send you a replacement jar of honey at no additional cost. Please send us your order details, and we'll take care of it right away." Always follow through on your promises to rebuild trust.

Use negative feedback as an opportunity to identify areas for improvement. If multiple customers point out the same issue, such as delayed shipping or unclear product descriptions, take proactive steps to address these problems. Communicate these improvements to your audience to show that you value their input. For example, "We've heard your feedback and are now using more secure packaging to ensure your candles arrive in perfect condition." Document these changes in your product updates or newsletters to keep your community informed.

Respond to negative comments publicly when possible. This shows other customers that you're proactive in resolving issues. For instance, if a customer leaves a critical comment on your Instagram post, reply with a polite and constructive response, such as, "We're sorry to hear about your experience and would love to make it right. Please send us a direct message so we can assist you further." Public responses demonstrate transparency and accountability. However, if the conversation gets too personal or sensitive, move it to private messages.

Lastly, know when to escalate or remove interactions. While constructive criticism is valuable, abusive or inappropriate comments should not be tolerated. Use platform tools to report or block users if necessary, but always prioritize professional and courteous communication. Keep records of these interactions for future reference or to learn from.

Using Feedback to Improve

Customer feedback, both positive and negative, is a goldmine of insights for your business. By actively listening to your customers and implementing their suggestions, you can refine your offerings, enhance the customer experience, and build a stronger brand.

Start by categorizing feedback to identify trends. For example, if several customers suggest offering smaller packaging options for your organic granola, consider introducing a trial-sized version. Similarly, if customers consistently praise a specific product, such as your lavender-scented candles, you might focus on promoting that item more prominently. Use software like HubSpot or simple spreadsheets to track feedback themes over time.

Conduct surveys to gather more structured feedback. Use tools like Google Forms or social media polls to ask customers about their preferences, experiences, and suggestions. For instance, a vegetable farmer could create a poll asking, "What new produce would you like to see at our booth this season? Options: heirloom tomatoes, sweet corn, or zucchini." Surveys show that you value customer opinions and are willing to adapt to meet their needs. Offer incentives like discount codes for completing surveys to boost participation.

Share how you're implementing feedback to keep your audience engaged. For example, a soap maker might post on Instagram, "Thanks to your feedback, we're excited to introduce our new unscented soap for sensitive skin! It'll be available at this weekend's market." Highlighting these changes not only strengthens customer relationships but also encourages more feedback in the future. Celebrate these updates through video content or live sessions to show the human side of your brand.

Use testimonials and positive reviews to reinforce your brand's credibility. Feature these on your website, social media, and marketing materials. For example, a bread baker might share a customer's review saying, "The best sourdough I've ever had! Perfectly crusty and delicious." Accompany the testimonial with a photo of the bread to create a compelling post. Consider a "Customer Stories" series where you spotlight different customers and their experiences with your products.

Advanced Engagement and Learning from Feedback

- **Interactive Q&A Sessions:** Host live sessions on platforms like Instagram Live or TikTok Live where customers can ask questions in real-time. This direct interaction not only answers queries but also builds community. For example, a microgreen grower could do a live session on "How to Use Microgreens in Your Diet" where viewers can ask about specific applications.

- **Feedback Loops:** Implement a system where feedback leads to action, which then gets communicated back to the customer base. If you change a recipe based on feedback, announce it with a "You Asked, We Listened" campaign. This shows responsiveness and can increase customer loyalty.

- **Beta Testing:** Before launching new products, invite loyal customers or followers to beta test them. This can be done through exclusive groups on social platforms or via email. Collect their feedback and use it to refine the product before a full release. For example, a candle maker might offer a few customers early access to a new scent profile.

- **Customer Advisory Boards:** For businesses with a strong community, consider forming a customer advisory board. This group can give regular feedback on product development, marketing strategies, or market experiences. It fosters a sense of ownership and involvement among your most engaged customers.

- **Analytics for Feedback:** Use analytics tools to see not just what customers say but how they interact with your content or website. High engagement on posts about sustainability might indicate a market trend you can leverage, like expanding your eco-friendly product line.

Closing Thoughts

Effectively handling customer inquiries and feedback is essential for building trust, improving your offerings, and fostering long-term relationships with your audience. By responding to comments and messages promptly, managing negative feedback with professionalism and empathy, leveraging feedback to drive improvements, and engaging in advanced interactions, you can enhance your brand's reputation and create a loyal customer base. Remember, every interaction with a customer is an opportunity to learn, grow, and strengthen your business. Through these strategies, you turn customer feedback into one of your most valuable assets for growth and development.

Part 5

Measuring and Growing Your Success

Chapter 13:

Understanding Analytics

Understanding analytics is essential for making informed decisions about your social media strategy. By tracking engagement, reach, and conversions, you can gain insights into what resonates with your audience and refine your approach to achieve better results. Analytics empower you to measure the effectiveness of your efforts, identify top-performing content, and continually improve your social media presence. In this chapter, we'll explore how to track key metrics, adjust your strategy based on data, leverage your best content to maximize impact, and delve into advanced analytics techniques for deeper insights.

Tracking Engagement, Reach, and Conversions

Analytics provide a wealth of data about your audience's interactions with your content. The three primary metrics to track are engagement, reach, and conversions. Each offers unique insights into how your audience is responding to your posts and how effectively your content is driving desired actions.

Engagement measures how actively your audience interacts with your content. This includes likes, comments, shares, saves, and clicks. For example, a baker might notice that posts featuring step-by-step baking tips receive more comments and shares than product showcase posts. High engagement indicates that your content resonates with your audience and encourages interaction. It's also crucial to look at the quality of engagement; comments with questions or feedback can guide content creation or highlight areas for customer service improvement.

Reach refers to the number of unique users who see your content. It's an important metric for assessing the visibility of your posts. For instance, a vegetable farmer promoting their market booth might find that posts with eye-catching visuals and local hashtags reach more users than text-heavy updates. Monitoring reach helps you identify the types of content that attract new viewers. Consider also looking at impressions for total views, which can sometimes differ from reach if users see your content multiple times.

Conversions track the actions users take after engaging with your content, such as visiting your website, signing up for a newsletter, or making a purchase. For example, a candle maker running an Instagram ad campaign might measure how many users clicked the "Shop Now" button and completed a purchase. Conversions are a key indicator of your content's ability to drive tangible results. To enhance this, set up conversion tracking in platforms like Google Analytics or through social media's native tools to connect online interactions directly to sales or other actions.

Use platform-specific analytics tools to monitor these metrics. Facebook Insights, Instagram Analytics, and Twitter Analytics provide detailed data about engagement, reach, and conversions. For multi-platform tracking, tools like Google Analytics or Hootsuite can consolidate data into a single dashboard, making it easier to compare performance across channels. Additionally, linking your website with social media for tracking via UTM parameters can provide precise data on how social traffic contributes to website actions.

Adjusting Your Strategy Based on Data

Analytics are most valuable when used to inform and refine your social media strategy. By analyzing the data, you can identify what's working, what isn't, and how to improve your approach. Regularly reviewing your metrics ensures that your strategy remains dynamic and aligned with your goals.

Start by comparing the performance of different types of content. For example, a soap maker might find that posts featuring behind-the-scenes videos of the soap-making process generate higher engagement than static product photos. Based on this insight, they could increase the frequency of video content to maintain audience interest. Use A/B testing to experiment with different content formats, captions, or calls to action to see what yields the best results.

Consider your audience demographics when analyzing data. For instance, a honey producer might discover that their audience skews younger on Instagram and older on Facebook. This information could influence the tone and style of their content on each platform, such as using trendy memes on Instagram and sharing educational articles on Facebook.

Segmenting your audience data can reveal further details about behavior and preferences, allowing for more targeted content.

Experiment with posting times and frequencies to optimize engagement. Analytics can reveal when your audience is most active, allowing you to schedule posts for maximum visibility. For example, a food truck operator might notice that posts published at noon receive higher engagement, as followers are likely browsing for lunch options. Adjusting your posting schedule accordingly can boost performance. Tools like Buffer or Sprout Social can automate this process based on your analytics.

Track the effectiveness of campaigns and promotions. For example, a jewelry maker running a two-week Valentine's Day promotion could monitor metrics like click-through rates and sales conversions to assess the campaign's success. If the data shows low engagement, they might tweak the offer or messaging mid-campaign to improve results. Use cohort analysis to see how different groups respond over time to your marketing efforts.

Identifying Top-Performing Content

Identifying and leveraging your top-performing content is a key strategy for maximizing your social media success. Your best-performing posts offer valuable insights into what resonates with your audience and can serve as a blueprint for future content.

Review your analytics to pinpoint posts with the highest engagement, reach, and conversions. For example, a microgreen grower might notice that a time-lapse video of their growing process consistently garners high likes and shares. This indicates that followers are interested in visually engaging and educational content. Look for patterns in content type, time of posting, or specific elements like hashtags or visuals that contribute to success.

Repurpose successful content to extend its lifespan and reach. For instance, a bread baker whose post featuring a sourdough recipe went viral could turn the recipe into a video tutorial or an infographic. Repurposing allows you to capitalize on the popularity of your best content while catering to different audience preferences. Consider creating a series or a content hub around a successful theme or product.

Use your top-performing content as inspiration for future posts. Analyze what made the content successful—whether it was the visuals, messaging, or timing—and apply those elements to new creations. For example, if a vegetable farmer's post about seasonal recipes performed well, they could create a series of similar posts highlighting different seasonal ingredients. This approach ensures your content strategy is data-driven.

Promote your best content to reach an even wider audience. Boosting top-performing posts on Facebook or Instagram ensures that they are seen by more users, increasing their impact. For example, a candle maker could boost a popular post showcasing their holiday gift sets to drive additional sales during the holiday season. Use targeted boosting to reach similar audiences or retarget those who've shown interest but haven't converted.

Track the long-term performance of top-performing content to gauge its ongoing impact. Some posts, such as educational articles or evergreen videos, can continue to attract engagement and drive traffic long after they are published. By understanding which content has lasting value, you can prioritize similar types of content in your strategy. Tools like Google Analytics can show you how long content continues to bring in traffic or conversions.

Advanced Analytics Techniques

- **Sentiment Analysis:** Use tools like Brandwatch or Mention to understand the sentiment behind comments and posts. This can help you gauge brand perception beyond mere engagement numbers. For example, positive sentiment around a new product launch can be as valuable as high engagement.

- **Funnel Analysis:** Track the customer journey from awareness to purchase. Platforms like Mixpanel or Amplitude can visualize how users move through each stage of interaction with your content. If many users drop off at the checkout stage, you might need to simplify your purchasing process.

- **Predictive Analytics:** Tools like IBM Watson or Google's AI offerings can predict future trends based on historical data. For instance, predicting which products will be popular in the upcoming season can help with inventory and marketing planning.

- **Social Listening:** Beyond your own pages, listen to conversations about your brand or industry on social media. This can reveal opportunities for new content or partnerships. Services like Hootsuite Insights can help you monitor these conversations in real-time.

- **Heatmaps and User Behavior:** For website interactions driven by social media, tools like Hotjar offer heatmaps showing where users click or how far they scroll. This can inform how you present information on your site to match user behavior from social media.

Closing Thoughts

Analytics are an essential tool for optimizing your social media strategy and achieving your business goals. By tracking engagement, reach, and conversions, you gain valuable insights into audience behavior and content performance. Using this data to adjust your strategy ensures that your efforts remain effective and aligned with your objectives. Identifying and leveraging top-performing content allows you to maximize your impact and continually refine your approach. With advanced analytics techniques, you can delve deeper into user behavior, predict trends, and listen to broader conversations around your brand. With a deep understanding of analytics, you can create a dynamic and data-driven social media presence that drives long-term success.

Chapter 14:

Scaling Your Business

Scaling your business is a pivotal step in achieving sustained growth and maximizing your potential. For farmers market vendors, this process often involves expanding beyond local markets, leveraging e-commerce and shipping, transitioning into full-time entrepreneurship, exploring new product lines, and maintaining brand integrity through growth. Scaling requires strategic planning, adaptability, and a willingness to invest in new opportunities. This chapter explores how to take your business to the next level while maintaining your core values and customer relationships.

Expanding Beyond Local Markets

Expanding beyond local markets allows you to reach new audiences and grow your customer base. While local markets are a great foundation, diversifying your sales channels and exploring regional or national opportunities can significantly increase your revenue and brand visibility.

One way to expand is by participating in larger regional markets or festivals. These events often attract bigger crowds and provide exposure to customers outside your immediate community. For example, a microgreen grower might secure a booth at a state fair, showcasing their products to thousands of attendees and gaining new wholesale clients in the process. Consider festivals themed around food, health, or sustainability, which align with your product offerings.

Another strategy is to establish partnerships with retailers or co-ops. For instance, a soap maker could approach local boutiques or gift shops about stocking their products. These partnerships not only generate additional income but also introduce your brand to a new customer demographic. Building relationships with retailers often requires providing samples, creating appealing packaging, and demonstrating a reliable production process. Look into artisanal or eco-friendly retail chains for a natural fit.

Expanding geographically through wholesale accounts is another option. Farmers and producers can work with restaurants, catering companies, or grocery stores that prioritize locally sourced goods. A honey producer, for example, might partner with farm-to-table restaurants in neighboring towns, offering their product as a premium ingredient for recipes or gift baskets. Develop a wholesale pricing strategy that maintains profitability while being attractive to buyers.

It's crucial to maintain the quality and authenticity of your products as you expand. Customers value the personal touch that small businesses bring, so ensure that scaling your operations doesn't compromise your brand's core values. For example, a bread baker scaling up production might invest in larger equipment without sacrificing the artisanal techniques that make their products unique. Regular quality checks and feedback loops with new customers can help maintain standards.

Leveraging E-commerce and Shipping

E-commerce is a game-changer for small businesses, allowing you to reach customers far beyond your local area. Setting up an online store enables you to generate sales 24/7 and cater to customers who may not be able to visit your farmers market booth in person.

Platforms like Shopify, WooCommerce, and Etsy make it easy to create a professional online store. Start by showcasing your best-selling products with high-quality photos and detailed descriptions. For example, a candle maker could include descriptions highlighting the natural ingredients and unique scents of their products, along with lifestyle photos showing the candles in cozy home settings. Ensure your site is mobile-friendly, considering a significant portion of shopping now occurs on mobile devices.

Shipping logistics are a critical component of e-commerce. Invest in durable, eco-friendly packaging that protects your products during transit while reinforcing your brand's values. For instance, a vegetable farmer offering CSA (Community Supported Agriculture) boxes might use recyclable boxes and include a handwritten thank-you note to create a memorable unboxing experience. Consider partnering with local artisans for packaging materials that align with your brand's aesthetic and ethos.

Offer multiple shipping options to accommodate customer preferences. Standard shipping may be sufficient for most orders, but expedited options can appeal to last-minute shoppers or gift buyers. A honey producer could promote their products as the perfect holiday gift, offering gift wrapping and express shipping during peak seasons. Use shipping software to manage rates, print labels, and track shipments efficiently, reducing the administrative burden.

E-commerce also provides opportunities to engage with customers digitally. Use email marketing to promote special offers, share recipes or tips related to your products, and announce new arrivals. For example, a soap maker might send a monthly newsletter featuring "Soap of the Month" promotions and behind-the-scenes stories about their crafting process. These interactions help maintain customer loyalty and encourage repeat purchases. Implement a loyalty program or subscription model to ensure recurring revenue.

Transitioning to Full-Time Entrepreneurship

Transitioning to full-time entrepreneurship is a significant milestone that requires careful planning and a solid foundation. For many farmers market vendors, this step involves scaling operations, securing consistent revenue streams, and committing to their business as a primary source of income.

Start by evaluating your current financial situation. Calculate your monthly expenses and income to determine whether your business can sustain your personal and professional needs. For instance, a food truck operator considering full-time entrepreneurship might analyze their busiest seasons, average sales per event, and potential for additional revenue through catering gigs. Create a financial buffer or emergency fund to handle unexpected expenses or dips in sales.

Diversify your income streams to reduce financial risk. This might include selling at multiple markets, launching an online store, or offering workshops and classes. A mushroom grower, for example, could supplement their market sales by hosting "Grow Your Own Mushrooms" workshops or selling grow kits online. Diversification ensures that your business remains resilient during slower periods. Explore opportunities like consulting or speaking engagements related to your area of expertise.

Invest in your business to support growth. This could mean purchasing better equipment, hiring additional staff, or renting a larger production space. A bread baker transitioning to full-time entrepreneurship might upgrade to commercial ovens to meet increased demand while maintaining quality. These investments are essential for scaling sustainably and effectively. Consider lease-to-own options or small business loans if capital upfront is a challenge.

Develop a long-term strategy that includes clear goals and milestones. For instance, a jewelry maker might set a goal to expand their online presence, grow their wholesale accounts, and double their annual revenue within three years. Having a roadmap helps you stay focused and measure progress. Regularly revisit and adjust your strategy based on market feedback and performance metrics.

Lastly, embrace the mindset of a full-time entrepreneur. Treat your business like a professional endeavor by maintaining a consistent schedule, setting boundaries, and continually seeking opportunities for growth. Networking with other full-time entrepreneurs and joining small business communities can provide valuable support and insights as you navigate this transition. Attend workshops or subscribe to business growth newsletters to keep learning and adapting.

Exploring New Product Lines

As your business scales, consider expanding your product lines to meet evolving customer demands and market trends:

- **Complementary Products:** If you sell honey, for instance, consider adding beeswax candles, lip balms, or skincare items. This not only uses by-products but also keeps customers within your brand ecosystem for more purchases.

- **Seasonal Offerings:** Create products that align with different times of the year. A jam and preserve maker might introduce special editions for holiday seasons or summer fruits, capitalizing on seasonal trends.

- **Customization and Personalization:** Offer customization options, like personalized labels or scents, which can command higher prices and create a unique buying experience. For example, a candle maker might offer to customize scents or packaging for weddings or corporate events.

- **Health and Specialty Products:** Cater to niche markets like gluten-free, vegan, or organic products. A bakery might introduce a line of health-focused baked goods, tapping into health trends and expanding their market.

- **Bundling:** Create product bundles that offer value and convenience. A microgreen grower could offer a "Chef's Kit" with various microgreens, recipes, and perhaps a small cutting tool, appealing to home cooks and professional chefs alike.

Maintaining Brand Integrity Through Growth

- **Stay True to Your Values:** As you grow, keep the mission, vision, and values that defined your brand. If sustainability was central to your brand, continue to source materials responsibly and communicate these efforts.

- **Customer Engagement:** Even with growth, maintain personal connections with your customers. Use social media to continue sharing stories, answering questions, and showing appreciation for customer loyalty.

- **Quality Control:** Implement systems or hire staff specifically for quality control as production scales. Regularly solicit customer feedback to ensure your products meet or exceed expectations.

- **Brand Consistency:** Whether expanding into new markets or launching new products, ensure that all branding elements (logo, packaging, tone) remain consistent to avoid diluting your brand identity.

- **Community Involvement:** Continue to be involved in local or industry events, sponsorships, or donations. This keeps your brand rooted in the community and supports your narrative as a business that cares.

Closing Thoughts

Scaling your business is a journey that requires strategic planning, adaptability, and a commitment to growth. By expanding beyond local markets, leveraging e-commerce and shipping, transitioning to full-time entrepreneurship, exploring new product lines, and maintaining brand integrity through growth, you can unlock new opportunities and achieve lasting success. Remember, the key to scaling is maintaining the quality and authenticity that made your business successful in the first place. With careful planning and a customer-focused approach, you can take your business to new heights while staying true to your brand's values and vision.

Chapter 15:

Staying Current in the Digital Age

The digital landscape evolves rapidly, and businesses must adapt to remain competitive. For farmers market vendors, staying current with social media trends, experimenting with new platforms, committing to continued learning, and embracing emerging technologies are critical to maintaining a strong online presence and connecting with customers. In this chapter, we'll explore strategies to keep your business ahead in the ever-changing digital age.

Keeping Up with Social Media Trends

Social media trends are constantly shifting, influenced by new features, audience behaviors, and cultural moments. Keeping up with these trends ensures that your content stays relevant and engaging, helping you maintain and grow your audience.

Start by regularly researching industry updates and changes to social media algorithms. Platforms like Instagram and Facebook frequently adjust how they prioritize content, impacting visibility and engagement. For example, a bread baker who learns that Instagram's algorithm favors Reels might shift their strategy to focus on creating short, engaging videos showcasing their baking process. Subscribe to newsletters from platforms or marketing blogs for updates.

Follow social media experts, industry leaders, and relevant hashtags to stay informed about emerging trends. Participate in webinars or join groups where professionals share tips and insights. For instance, a soap maker could benefit from a marketing group discussing the latest features on Pinterest and how to optimize product pins for discovery. Engage with these communities by asking questions or even contributing your insights.

Embrace trending content formats and themes that align with your brand. For example, if a viral TikTok challenge involves showcasing "behind-the-scenes" moments, a microgreen grower could join by creating a video showing the planting and harvesting process. Participating in trends not only increases visibility but also demonstrates that your business is attuned to current conversations. Remember to adapt these trends to fit your brand's narrative, like using a trending hashtag to highlight your sustainability practices.

Analyze how trends resonate with your audience. While it's tempting to jump on every trend, prioritize those that align with your brand values and goals. For example, a honey producer might focus on sustainability trends by creating content about eco-friendly packaging or the importance of bees in the ecosystem, which ties back to their mission. Use analytics to see if these trends drive engagement or sales, and adjust your approach accordingly.

Experimenting with New Platforms

Emerging platforms often offer unique opportunities to connect with audiences in innovative ways. Experimenting with these platforms allows you to stay ahead of the curve and discover untapped potential for your business.

Start by exploring platforms that cater to your target audience. For example, younger audiences are more active on TikTok, while Pinterest attracts users seeking inspiration and DIY ideas. A candle maker might find success on TikTok by sharing creative candle-making tutorials, while a jewelry maker could thrive on Pinterest with visually appealing pins showcasing their designs. Research each platform's user base demographics to ensure alignment with your market.

Test the waters by posting a few pieces of content and analyzing the response. For instance, a food truck operator could create a series of short, engaging videos on TikTok featuring their cooking process and customer reactions. By monitoring views, likes, and comments, they can gauge whether the platform is worth investing more time and effort. Use platform-specific analytics to track performance metrics.

Collaborate with influencers or creators who are already established on new platforms. For example, a vegetable farmer looking to break into YouTube might partner with a food blogger to create a cooking video featuring their produce. This collaboration not only introduces your brand to a new audience but also leverages the influencer's credibility. Such partnerships can be formal, with agreed terms, or informal, like mutual shout-outs.

Be patient and persistent. New platforms often require time to build a following and understand what content performs best. For example, a soap maker experimenting with Pinterest might spend several months refining their pin designs and learning how to optimize descriptions for search visibility. Consistency and adaptability are key to succeeding on new platforms. Regularly review your strategy and pivot based on what you learn from engagement and feedback.

Investing in Continued Learning

The digital world is ever-evolving, and staying competitive requires a commitment to ongoing education. Investing in your knowledge and skills ensures that you can adapt to changes and make the most of new opportunities.

Take advantage of online courses, workshops, and certifications to deepen your understanding of digital marketing. Platforms like Coursera, LinkedIn Learning, and HubSpot offer courses on topics such as social media strategy, SEO, and analytics. For example, a honey producer could take a course on e-commerce optimization to improve their online store's performance. Set a goal to complete at least one course per quarter to keep your skills sharp.

Attend industry conferences and networking events to stay informed about the latest tools and strategies. For instance, a bread baker might participate in a food industry trade show featuring sessions on social media marketing for artisanal products. These events provide valuable insights and opportunities to connect with other professionals. Look for virtual events if travel is not feasible, which often have a broader reach and lower costs.

Learn from your peers by joining online communities or forums. Engage in discussions, ask questions, and share your experiences. For example, a vegetable farmer could join a Facebook group for farmers market vendors to exchange tips on marketing and customer engagement. Peer learning fosters collaboration and keeps you informed about what works for others. Platforms like Reddit or Slack channels can be great for niche industry discussions.

Invest time in experimenting with new tools and technologies. For instance, a candle maker could explore social media scheduling tools like Buffer or Later to streamline their posting process and free up time for creative tasks. Testing different tools helps you identify those that best suit your business needs. Keep an eye on emerging tech like AI for content creation or VR for experiential marketing.

Embracing Emerging Technologies

- **AI and Automation:** Utilize AI tools for content generation, customer service via chatbots, or personalized marketing. For example, a farmer could use AI to predict crop yield or customer buying patterns, optimizing their market strategy.
- **Augmented Reality (AR):** Implement AR for product visualization. A jewelry maker could allow customers to see how a piece looks on them through an AR app, enhancing the online shopping experience.
- **Virtual Reality (VR):** Create immersive experiences like virtual tours of your farm or market setup. This can be particularly engaging for educational content or to give urban customers a feel of rural life.

- **Blockchain for Traceability:** Use blockchain technology for transparency in your supply chain, which can be a significant selling point for consumers interested in food origin and quality. For instance, tracking honey from hive to jar.

- **Voice Search Optimization:** With the rise of smart speakers, optimize your content for voice search. This might mean focusing on conversational keywords if you're running an online shop.

Commitment to a Mindset of Continuous Improvement

- **Regular Reflection:** Set aside time each week or month to reflect on your progress, identify areas for growth, and set new goals. For example, a jewelry maker might review their social media analytics quarterly, identify content types with the highest engagement, and plan future campaigns accordingly.

- **Adaptability:** Be willing to pivot strategies based on what you learn from your experiments and feedback. If a new feature like Instagram's shopping tags doesn't work as expected, reassess and try different approaches.

- **Feedback Loops:** Establish mechanisms to get continuous feedback from your customers, whether through social media polls, direct messages, or review requests. Use this feedback to refine your offerings and communication.

- **Innovation Culture:** Encourage your team, if you have one, to bring forward new ideas or technologies they've encountered. A culture of innovation keeps everyone engaged and proactive in adapting to digital changes.

Closing Thoughts

Staying current in the digital age requires vigilance, experimentation, and a commitment to ongoing learning. By keeping up with social media trends, exploring new platforms, embracing emerging technologies, and investing in your knowledge, you can maintain a competitive edge and continually adapt to changes in the digital landscape. These efforts not only enhance your online presence but also ensure that your business remains relevant, innovative, and successful. With a forward-thinking approach, you can navigate the ever-evolving digital world and thrive in the long term. Remember, the digital age offers endless opportunities for those willing to learn and adapt.

Conclusion

The journey to building and maintaining a successful presence in the digital marketplace is one filled with opportunities, challenges, and immense potential for growth. By leveraging the tools and strategies outlined in this book, you can create a thriving business that not only stands out but also connects deeply with your customers. Let's reflect on the path forward, starting with your journey in the digital marketplace, taking small steps to achieve big success, empowering your brand for the future, fostering resilience, and envisioning a community-driven approach to digital marketing.

Your Journey in the Digital Marketplace

The digital marketplace offers a unique opportunity for farmers market vendors and small businesses to expand their reach beyond traditional boundaries. What was once limited to in-person interactions at a weekend market is now accessible to a global audience through social media, e-commerce platforms, and innovative marketing strategies. This shift opens new doors for creativity, connection, and growth.

As you navigate this journey, it's important to remember that authenticity is your greatest asset. Customers are drawn to brands that share their values, tell meaningful stories, and provide exceptional products. For example, a vegetable farmer who shares weekly updates about their sustainable farming practices not only educates their audience but also builds trust and loyalty. Transparency and consistency lay the foundation for lasting relationships with your customers.

The digital marketplace is also dynamic and ever-changing. Algorithms shift, new platforms emerge, and consumer preferences evolve. Staying adaptable and committed to learning ensures that your business remains relevant. For instance, a soap maker who initially relied solely on Instagram might explore TikTok to tap into a younger demographic, diversifying their audience and opportunities.

Don't underestimate the importance of community in the digital space. Engage with other vendors, local organizations, and influencers to amplify your reach and build a supportive network. For example, a honey producer collaborating with a local chef to create recipe content for social media not only benefits both parties but also provides valuable content for their shared audiences. Collaboration fosters growth and strengthens your position in the digital marketplace.

Ultimately, your journey in the digital marketplace is about creating meaningful connections and delivering value. By staying true to your mission and embracing the tools available, you can carve out a space where your brand thrives, and your customers feel inspired to support you.

Small Steps to Big Success

Success in the digital age often begins with small, deliberate steps. While the prospect of scaling your business and mastering digital marketing might seem overwhelming, focusing on incremental progress ensures sustainable growth. Each step builds on the last, creating a strong foundation for long-term success.

Start by setting achievable goals. For example, a jewelry maker might aim to increase their Instagram following by 10% over three months by posting consistently and engaging with followers. Breaking larger objectives into manageable tasks allows you to measure progress and celebrate milestones along the way.

Embrace experimentation as part of the process. Try new content formats, test different posting schedules, and explore platforms outside your comfort zone. For instance, a bread baker might experiment with Instagram Reels to showcase the baking process in action. If one strategy doesn't work, adjust and try again. Each experiment provides valuable insights that inform your approach.

Consistency is key to building trust and visibility. Regularly posting high-quality content, responding to comments, and maintaining a cohesive brand voice demonstrate your reliability and commitment to your audience. Over time, these small actions compound, creating a loyal customer base that supports your business growth.

Leverage analytics to refine your strategy. Pay attention to metrics like engagement, reach, and conversions to understand what resonates with your audience. For example, a food truck operator might notice that posts featuring customer testimonials perform better than menu updates. Using this insight, they can prioritize testimonial content to drive higher engagement.

Remember that success is not linear. There will be challenges and setbacks, but each experience contributes to your growth and resilience. By focusing on small, actionable steps, you can achieve significant results and build a business that thrives in the digital age.

Empowering Your Brand for the Future

Empowering your brand for the future involves adopting a forward-thinking mindset and staying proactive in a constantly evolving landscape. The steps you take today lay the groundwork for tomorrow's success, so it's essential to remain adaptable, innovative, and customer-focused.

Invest in continued learning to stay ahead of trends and technologies. Attend workshops, take online courses, and engage with industry leaders to deepen your knowledge. For example, a candle maker might enroll in a digital marketing course to better understand SEO and e-commerce strategies, enhancing their online store's performance. Staying informed ensures that your brand remains competitive.

Focus on sustainability and scalability. As your business grows, evaluate how you can maintain quality and authenticity while meeting increased demand. For instance, a honey producer expanding their operations might invest in eco-friendly packaging solutions that align with their brand's commitment to sustainability. Scaling responsibly ensures that your brand's values remain intact.

Adapt to new technologies and platforms to meet your audience where they are. For example, a soap maker might explore augmented reality (AR) to allow customers to visualize how their products fit into their daily routines. Embracing innovation keeps your brand relevant and enhances the customer experience.

Empower your team and collaborators to contribute to your brand's success. Whether it's hiring staff, partnering with influencers, or working with local organizations, building a strong network of support allows you to focus on growth and strategic planning. For instance, a bread baker partnering with a digital marketer can create more effective campaigns while dedicating time to perfecting their craft.

Finally, stay true to your vision and mission. Your brand's authenticity and passion are what resonate most with customers. By continually refining your approach and staying connected to your purpose, you empower your brand to not only survive but thrive in the ever-changing digital marketplace.

Fostering Resilience

Resilience is crucial in the digital world where change is the only constant. Here's how to cultivate resilience:

- **Prepare for Digital Disruptions:** Have contingency plans for platform changes, social media outages, or shifts in consumer behavior. For instance, if Instagram changes its algorithm, a microgreen grower might quickly shift focus to Pinterest or YouTube to maintain visibility.
- **Diversify Your Digital Presence:** Don't rely on a single platform. Spread your efforts across multiple channels to mitigate risks. A candle maker might maintain an active presence

on Instagram, Pinterest, and a blog, ensuring they reach different segments of their audience.

- **Learn from Setbacks:** Each challenge or failure is an opportunity to learn. If a promotional campaign doesn't yield expected results, analyze why and use that knowledge to improve future strategies.
- **Embrace Customer Feedback:** Use negative feedback constructively to improve your products and services. This not only shows resilience but also builds customer trust as they see their input leads to real changes.

Envisioning a Community-Driven Approach

The future of digital marketing for farmers market vendors lies in fostering a community-driven approach:

- **User-Generated Content:** Encourage customers to share their experiences with your products. For example, a soap maker could run a monthly challenge where customers share creative ways to use their soaps, using a specific hashtag. This not only promotes your products but also builds a community around your brand.
- **Loyalty Programs:** Develop programs that reward engagement and purchases, turning casual buyers into brand advocates. A vegetable farmer might offer points for social shares, reviews, or repeat purchases, redeemable for discounts or exclusive products.
- **Interactive Community Spaces:** Create or participate in forums, groups, or social media groups where your community can interact, share ideas, and learn from each other. A honey producer could start a beekeeping forum where enthusiasts can discuss bee health and share tips, with the business providing expert advice.

- **Local Partnerships:** Continue to weave your digital presence with local initiatives. Participate in community events, sponsor local projects, or collaborate with schools for educational programs. These actions strengthen your community ties and enhance your brand's local relevance.

- **Sustainability Focus:** Make sustainability a central theme of your community engagement. Share your sustainable practices, educate on environmental issues, and encourage community-wide initiatives like local clean-ups or gardening projects. This not only aligns with many consumers' values but also positions your brand as a leader in eco-conscious practices.

The digital age offers endless possibilities for farmers market vendors and small businesses to grow, connect, and succeed. By embracing the journey, taking small steps toward big success, empowering your brand for the future, fostering resilience, and envisioning a community-driven approach to digital marketing, you can create a lasting impact in your industry. The tools, strategies, and insights shared in this book are just the beginning. With dedication, adaptability, and a commitment to your values, your business has the potential to flourish in ways you never imagined. The future is bright—and it starts with the steps you take today. Remember, in the digital marketplace, every interaction is a chance to grow, every feedback an opportunity to improve, and every day a new beginning for innovation and connection.

About the Author

Bill Davenport is a seasoned entrepreneur, retired Navy Chief, and the driving force behind Anchored Market Ventures, LLC, a company dedicated to empowering farmers market vendors, craft show vendors, and festival vendors to thrive in their local markets. With a passion for fostering community connections, Bill runs farmers markets across the Florida Panhandle, managing events that range in size from 15 to over 125 vendors. His work emphasizes bringing together local farmers, growers, producers, and makers to create vibrant hubs of commerce and community.

Bill's expertise in social media marketing and digital branding has made him a trusted resource for small business owners navigating the complexities of the digital age. Through his platforms on YouTube, Facebook, Instagram, TikTok, X (formerly Twitter), and his website, www.anchoredmarketventures.com, Bill shares actionable strategies and insights to help vendors stand out and succeed. Whether it's designing a visually appealing booth, crafting compelling social media content, or leveraging analytics to refine a marketing strategy, Bill's guidance is tailored to the unique challenges faced by market vendors.

Bill is also the author of ***Farmers Market Success: A Comprehensive Guide For Vendors***, an A to Z guide for new vendors, seasoned vendors, and those looking to become a vendor. This comprehensive resource provides valuable insights and practical advice for navigating every aspect of the farmers market experience, making it an essential read for anyone in the industry.

In addition to his hands-on market management and social media expertise, Bill is the host of the weekly ***Vendor's Edge Podcast***. This podcast is a cornerstone of his mission to empower vendors, offering practical advice, success stories, and in-depth discussions on topics ranging from branding to customer engagement. The *Vendor's Edge Podcast* has become a go-to resource for vendors looking to elevate their businesses and connect with a like-minded community.

Bill's journey from Navy service to market management is fueled by his unwavering dedication to supporting local economies and celebrating the creativity and hard work of small business owners. His leadership and innovative approach have not only transformed farmers markets into thriving ecosystems but have also inspired countless vendors to pursue their entrepreneurial dreams.

When he's not managing markets or creating content, Bill is passionate about connecting communities and championing the importance of supporting local businesses. Through Anchored Market Ventures, LLC, and his various platforms, Bill continues to make a lasting impact, helping vendors navigate the ever-changing marketplace with confidence and success.

Made in the USA
Columbia, SC
04 June 2025

58747745R00070